The Mask Handbook

'A very readable and usable book, it will be useful for students
and teachers, not only in training for the use of mask but for
developing skills in devising and performance skills. The book
demystifies much which has become the province of the
initiated and reserved for those in the know and is written by
someone with comprehensive and respected experience as
a writer, director and performer.'

Anne Fenton, *General Adviser Drama,*
West Sussex LEA

In *The Mask Handbook: A practical guide*, Europe's leading mask
director and co-founder of the Trestle Theatre Company sets out to
demystify the process of using masks. In an age of bland realism
on television and technological excess in film, masks have the ability
to truly play the fundamental game of theatre – the suspension of
disbelief. They ask the audience to participate in the theatrical process
in the way children do, with a desire to believe in the simple transformation of actor into character, and to connect their imaginations to
those of the actors.

Full of simple explanations and written by a director with over 25 years experience of writing for, directing and acting in masks, this book includes:

- an introduction to the origin of masks
- advice on preparing, making and using masks
- tips on writing, devising and directing mask work
- lots of fun and effective practical exercises.

This accessible and inspiring handbook will empower teachers, directors and actors to fully explore the world of the mask.

Toby Wilsher co-founded Trestle Theatre Company in 1981. For 23 years he was an actor, writer, maker, designer and director for Trestle, seeing his work performed in 31 countries. Since 2004 he is a freelance director, writer and corporate trainer.

The Mask Handbook

A practical guide

Toby Wilsher

Routledge

Taylor & Francis

LONDON AND NEW YORK

First published 2007
by Routledge
2 Park Square, Milton Park, Abingdon, Oxon OX14 4RN

Simultaneously published in the USA and Canada
by Routledge
711 Third Avenue, New York, NY 10017

*Routledge is an imprint of the Taylor & Francis Group,
an informa business*

Designed and typeset in Univers and Avant Garde
by Keystroke, 28 High Street, Tettenhall, Wolverhampton
Printed and bound in Great Britain
by TJI Digital, Padstow, Cornwall

British Library Cataloguing in Publication Data
A catalogue record for this book is available from the British Library

Library of Congress Cataloging in Publication Data
Wilsher, Toby.
The mask handbook : a practical guide / by Toby Wilsher.
p. cm.
Includes index.
1. Masks–Handbooks, manuals, etc. 2. Acting–Handbooks,
manuals, etc. I. Title.
PN2071.M37W55 2006
391.4'34–dc22
2006015187

ISBN10: 0–415–41436–9 (hbk)
ISBN10: 0–415–41437–7 (pbk)
ISBN10: 0–203–96779–8 (ebk)

ISBN13: 978–0–415–41436–4 (hbk)
ISBN13: 978–0–415–41437–1 (pbk)
ISBN13: 978–0–203–96779–9 (ebk)

For Gill and Barry

Contents

9 DEVELOPING TIME ON STAGE   135

10 THE HALF MASK   145

11 OTHER MASK TYPES   157

12 MASK DESIGN AND MAKING   163

    Contact information   177
    Bibliography   181
    Index   183

Illustrations

Acknowledgements

My long journey working in mask theatre has been accompanied by many wonderful people who all contributed to my experience and understanding of the ways of the mask. Of particular note were my co-collaborators at Middlesex University, London, Alan Riley, Sally Cook and Peter Walsingham, where we explored masks under the inspirational tutelage of John Wright. Together we formed Trestle Theatre Company, and were joined by Joff Chafer shortly afterwards. This core team discovered much together as we wrote, produced and toured the shows. And of course the company relied heavily on its company manager, Penny Mayes, who sent us to some very interesting places, and felt as fired up about masks as we all did, and on its highly resourceful set-builder and Production Manager, Mark Wilsher.

I am indebted to the many actors who found themselves encased in plastic or plaster for months on end, actors who set such a high benchmark of mask performance: James Greaves, Amanda Owen, Nicky Fearn, Simon Grover, Steve Harper, Steve Grihault, Roz Paul, Abigail Dulay, Sarah Moore, Jenny Hutchinson, Jason Webb, Thomasina Carlyle, Sarah Thom, Georgina Lamb, Paul Hunter . . . There are many more and I apologise to those I haven't mentioned.

Also a big thank you to the crews who travelled with us, who added to the mask experience creatively through the sound and light operation of the shows, as vital an ingredient as any other.

I am also indebted to some inspirational mask-makers. Apart from the original team at Trestle, I thank Russell Dean, Mike Chase and Ninian Kinnear Wilson.

My journey started when my mother took me to see the Moving Picture Mime Show in 1977. I was 18, and it blew me away. To Toby Sedgwick, Paul Filipiak and David Gaines, a huge thank you.

I never met him or trained with him, but everything that was starting in the late 1970s came from one man – Jacques Lecoq.

Introduction

The impetus behind this book is my desire to both demystify and reclaim the mask in theatre. Most of the literature available for the student or teacher is academic in tone, either historical or anthropological, and the theatre-based textbooks that offer training are hard to come by and, in my experience, overwhelming in their complexity. The wonderful thing about the full mask is its simplicity.

There are many books and articles that focus on the half mask, whether it is Gordon Craig's journal *The Mask* in the early twentieth century, or John Rudlin's (1994) exploration of Commedia dell'arte. Masks in general have often become the domain of the academic and though what they have written is interesting, it is of little use to someone actually trying to put on a show. This book fills in the gaps, showing the teacher, actor, writer or director how to bring a full mask alive onstage, how to provoke the performer into creating truthful characters and devising quality material. It is also intended to encourage the creators of theatre to consider the mask as part of their armoury, one of any number of tools in a toolkit that, in an age of cinema and television, and of realism on stage, has often been overlooked.

A form of language has built up around the mask that distances it from its true function – to engage and entertain an audience through the apparent transformation of actor into character – and has confused the theatrical mask with the masks studied by anthropologists. Anthropological masks have instigated many books of study, indeed, entire conferences have talked about nothing else. But there is a fundamental difference between the use of these sacred masks, and the masks we see on stage. But since the history of the mask is one initially of a sacred experience, this has skewed people's perceptions. I intend this book to be plain speaking, 'unmasking the mask'.

I knew little about masks when I went to see the Moving Picture Mime Show back in 1977. I saw a sketch called 'The Examination', an observation of three students and a teacher during an exam. It was very, very funny, and ultimately very moving. But what captivated me most about the piece was the way it connected with me. I felt utterly engrossed in the action, but also that I was in some way contributing to the event. My imagination was required. What's more, the experience of the piece was different for other people, since their memories of examinations had been different. They knew different people akin to the characters we were watching. And the characters had different voices, since we were all listening to our own vocabulary, interpreting the movements and gestures of the characters in our own voices. This experience led me to a training that explored mask theatre, and then on to form Trestle Theatre Company. Every show I worked on for 23 years sought to discover something new about how the mask worked, the context in which they could be used, and ways in which we could bring their magic to a wider audience.

Masks have often been at the forefront of popular theatre, a folk art that has had its place in the general consciousness of the culture. While it is often silent, it is not dumb. Mask theatre past and present is rich in emotion, narrative, humour, tragedy, metaphor, symbolism, political and social debate. It certainly has its place in the twenty-first century, and I hope this book encourages more participants to don the mask and connect with the imagination of the audience.

Figure 0 *Hanging Around*, Trestle Theatre Company

CHAPTER 1

Masks!? In the Twenty-first Century!?

A brief polemic: *Part One*

In the 1950s and 1960s, the way stories were presented to us was subtly different. Theatre was dominated by well-made plays that took place in rooms, and many films followed the same route, or at least had a relatively static camera. By and large the theatre was all about naturalism, or at least a realistic style of acting. Cinema did realism very well – much of the power of cinema is based in its ability to convince us that what we are seeing is real. The power of the edit suite was limited, and the movement of the camera was a complicated business. The bravura moments in the work of directors like David Lean or Orson Welles were often linked to the startling way they managed to move the camera. Above all, radio was at its peak as a means of telling stories and presenting plays.

A principal change since the 1960s is that we have become much more of a visually literate culture, through our exposure to television, cinema and advertising. If we compare these media over this period, we can see the way stories or information is communicated to us has become visually more sophisticated and witty, presupposing an understanding of the rules. Advertising can tell us a full story with five three-second cuts, while television is happy to employ the full range of techniques available to the editor in the edit suite, or to the director in terms of their ability to move the camera, freeze the action, isolate action, vary the speeds of action, split the screen, vary the way sound-track is used, changing volume and intensity, starting points etc. Cinema too has evolved, for good or bad, to utilise a broad range of technical tools to constantly keep the camera and the picture moving. Theatre has also evolved many exciting ways of presenting stories and ideas, though sadly these are rarely in evidence when one visits what one could term 'the mainstream'. The cutting-edge aspects of television and film are often very visible and accepted, but the same elements in theatre are generally confined to the fringe or the avant garde. In mainstream theatre, by and large, actors are doing exactly what they were doing in the 1950s – speaking beautifully and not bumping into the furniture. Mainstream directors too often consider the script as being the last part of the process, a sacrosanct item not to be tampered with. The result is Peter Brook's 'Dead Theatre', what I call 'Tribute Theatre', which, like the ubiquitous tribute bands, aims to reproduce the author's initial intentions to the letter, irrespective of when and for whom it was written. The danger is that Dead Theatre is alienating its audience.

Ruth Mackenzie, in a speech in 2003 at the Chichester Festival Theatre, commented on how, in all aspects of British culture, every-body sought out the 'new' – the latest fashions, music, art, the hot film, the new magazine etc. Except theatre. Mention the 'new' in theatre and there is often a sharp intake of breath. Why is this? Because, for all the developments in so many different areas of performance and culture, mainstream theatre has undergone virtually no change at all.

The so-called fringe is full of experimentation, new forms and spaces. And continental theatre is rich in visual spectacle, multi media events, aerialists combining with fireworks, wonderful puppetry, dazzling dance. Directors like Robert Lepage, Robert Wilson, Pina Bausch and Julie Taymor have created work that bristles with invention, imagination, popular appeal and an understanding of the materials and technologies available. Opera has not been slow to realise the rich forms that now exist, to find new ways of telling old stories, with designers and directors having free rein to their imaginations, with dazzling technology contributing to the spectacle, and large-scale operas taking place in the Royal Albert Hall. Circus has found a new way of presenting the marvels and skills of human invention with Cirque du Soleil leading the field. Mainstream theatre often seems lumpen and outdated by comparison.   ·

What is the mainstream? Is it the theatre for the keen but nervous – keen to go to the theatre, but nervous of something untoward happening to them while they are there? Is it theatre that is safe, that takes no risks? The worst that can be said about visiting the theatre is that when you leave, your mood hasn't changed. Is this the mainstream? Obviously there isn't a catch-all, a generalisation, but there is definitely a style of theatre, what one could describe as 'room' theatre, that asks very little of its audience other than that they turn up and not rustle their sweet papers. What theatre needs, I would argue, now, at the beginning of the twenty-first century, are more masks and more puppets.

Masks are a folk art for the simple reason that they have an immediacy and connection with their audience that crosses cultural boundaries and leaps the centuries. Masks play the essential game of theatre, and are an antidote to the technological excess of film or the bland realism of television. They require the audience to watch as they did when they were children, wide-eyed and believing, to suspend their disbelief, their adult sensibilities and their twenty-first-century cynicism. In an age far removed from the belief in miracles and transformation, masks allow us to enter into a mind state where we witness performers creating an otherness, a complete world that is somehow not of this world and yet that is recognisable and believable. Masks offer us a spiritual experience when we least expect one – not in a religious sense, but certainly a feeling of being taken outside of our selves, a chance to lose oneself in the world of our imagination, much like listening to a great piece of transcendental music.

Obviously, masks are not to everybody's taste. Some people find them, along with puppets, crude and shallow, a gimmick from the carnival or circus. I have seen some very bad mask theatre, but there again, I've seen some brilliant stuff. If you see a couple of bad shows, you are likely to dismiss the entire art form, whereas that would not be true of theatre itself. You don't stop going to the cinema because you see a bad film. The trouble is, when masks are bad, they are very, very bad. The onlookers quickly become angry, as there is nothing but a dumb show for them to watch. There is no connection. So while I would advocate an increased use of the mask and puppet in twenty-first-century theatre, it has to be good, otherwise it will be dismissed very quickly. This book is a practical guide intended to assist in the creation of quality work.

What form these masks may take is completely open. Whereas masks from past significant periods in theatre history have created a range of stock characters, such as the masks of Greek, Roman, Commedia dell'arte or Noh theatre, the exploration and experimentation in theatre today is a vastly accelerated process, with diversity and unique-ness, rather than conformity being the goal. In the past, and still today in some cultures, such as Bali, the masks used were clearly from one 'family', even when spread over a large geographical area. The sixteenth-century Commedia family of masks could be seen from Calais to Naples, the same masks reproduced with little variation by different mask-makers. That was its strength. But today western Europe alone contains a wide range of styles and forms that come and go with the ebb and flow of creators and designers. Masks have ceased to become just a simple representation of the face, but now include inanimate objects, wild cartoon designs, grotesque caricatures etc. The single unifier of all these styles is the technique needed to bring them to life and to live in the audience's imagination.

Figure 1.1 Company of Angels, Horse and Bamboo

CHAPTER 2

Where do Our Masks Come From?

The history of masks is also the history of theatre itself, so to catalogue the entire backstory of the mask is a serious undertaking. Many books can be found that undertake such a task, so I do not wish to reproduce them here. But there are several interesting factors I wish to cover. First, what do we actually mean by 'the mask', and second, what are the roots of the masks we see and use today?

What is a mask?

There are few words that have as many connotations as the word 'mask'. The word conjures up a vast range of images, from the Greek masks of comedy and tragedy, to African ritual, the mask of Zorro and Jim Carrey in *The Mask* (1994). Throw into that the clown's red nose, the many protective masks – a gas mask, a fencer's mask, a surgeon's mask – and it becomes a daunting task to define them all.

The word has both positive and negative meanings. As a noun, the interpretation covers a host of artefacts with a range of uses, from the utilitarian such as the mask that protects, like sunglasses or a welder's helmet, to the theatrical. Masks are worn by wrestlers, criminals, party-goers, festival celebrants. They appear on the heads of the Ku Klux Klan, on a Muslim bride and groom, on 'trick-or-treaters'. But as a verb, the negative aspect comes to the fore, suggesting concealment or deceit, either of the face or person, or of emotions or intentions.

Would you consider a woman's make-up to be a mask? How about Buster Keaton's immobile face? Maybe a full set of beard and moustache hides something. Masks can be so many things – decorative, useful, concealing or revealing. They can threaten, entertain, protect or unify. Is a definition possible?

Loosely one can say that a mask is a covering of part or all of the face or body that can disguise, protect or transform. The defining of masks and the exposition of their power have resulted in vast amounts of writings from academics and theorists, so much so that it is easy to lose sight of what the mask is simply about. This book is about masks that have a job to do, and that job is to entertain. Therefore my definition of this type of mask is simple.

It transforms.

From this simple function one can start layering on all the reasons, methods, applications and so on. I shall break this down into two straightforward worlds, the sacred and the secular.

Under the heading of sacred come all the masks where the society in which they are used truly believe that the transformation that takes place when somebody dons a mask is magic, and that both the wearer and the mask itself are imbued with that magic. This could include the wearer as well, who is transformed mentally by wearing a mask, into a state of trance.

In a secular society, all the above is not true, and if people say that it is, then I would suggest that the experience of watching or wearing a mask is an excuse or a metaphor for something else to do with that person, such as a longing for some belief, or a form of psychotherapy that is fulfilling a need. The magic that is intangible, but that exists when people in a secular society watch masks comes from one source – the imagination of the audience.

Historically, therefore, while masks have always begun in sacred societies, from the earliest days, supporting a belief system for a myriad of religious beliefs, it is interesting to note that when those same societies took on more secular beliefs, the use of the mask started to enter the world of entertainment. The Greeks, for example.

There are sacred societies today for whom the mask is a principal part of the ritual structure of the religion, such as on the continent of Africa. In Europe, masks appear in many festivals, particularly in central European countries such as Austria and Switzerland, where the mask is part of a celebration that has its roots in past belief systems, but the festival now exists as part of the celebratory facet of that society, either as a tourist attraction, or part of the communal glue that holds them together, and sets them apart from other communities.

In our secular society, the use and understanding of the mask, outside of entertainment, has become wrapped up in superstition, which one could argue is what happens to a society when it ditches its religious beliefs, beliefs central to that society. In Christianity, Roman Catholics believe in transubstantiation, the turning of wine and bread into the blood and flesh of Jesus Christ. In Anthony Burgess's novel *Earthly Powers* (1980), a missionary is killed and eaten by tribesmen he had converted, because they truly believed what he was saying, and to eat him, as the priest suggests we 'eat' Jesus when we take the sacrament, was a good thing. This example of sacred beliefs within a secular society coming into contact with the unflinching beliefs in a sacred society has some resonance in how masks are sometimes perceived today.

In a sacred society, a mask is totemic, shamanic, an object linked to deity, a liminal tool that stands at the threshold of the world they know and the world they don't. Masks in this society are unequivocal, unambiguous and never metaphoric. In a secular society such as Britain, masks are used for entertainment. But there is still a desire within the society for the comfort of total faith and belief, and to this end masks are being reimbued with a sacred magic, and that magic defined by academe. The result is therefore a great confusion about masks in our society. Some are fearful of them, of their transformative power, of both wearer and watcher. For some years there has been resistance to masks in many schools, where the head or drama teacher knew the Keith Johnstone approach to masks in his book *Impro* (1979). Here Johnstone advocated the use of the trance for unlocking the creative power of both mask and actor, but such a method was deemed unsafe and unsuitable for children. The critical response to Peter Hall's *Oresteia* (1981) at the National Theatre principally denounced the use of the masks as being outmoded and irrelevant. Yet an audience responsive to mask theatre has the possibility of enjoying the most profound theatrical experience they will ever have. This is because the transforming power of the mask, in the audience's imagination, takes them back to childhood beliefs, when one listened open-mouthed to a story or watched a puppet show with wide-eyed credulity. But this power is not specific, not defined. Nor should it be feared. It is, ultimately, the power of the imagination. This imaginative leap, the suspension of disbelief at the heart of the theatrical experience, differs from the unquestioning faith and total belief of a member of a sacred society. There is a willingness to join in, to play the game. There is acknowledgement of the pretence but a joy in the exercise. Theatre has always transformed the world outside, and challenged the audience to accept that transformation. Masks in theatre have historically been at the forefront of that transformation. Sacred masks and masks for entertainment might seem poles apart, but in the transformative power they wield, and the personal connection with their audience we can see that today's masks have their roots in an older and more spiritual age.

Finally, before we examine further where the mask has come from, let us consider what it does, why it existed. That various societies and cultures had previously encountered the transformative power of the mask is understood. Why carry it on to the stage? Peter Hall, founder of the Royal Shakespeare Company and director of the National Theatre for many years, is also known for his staging of Greek dramas in masks. In his book, *Exposed by the Mask* (2000) (not actually a mask book!) he suggests that audiences crave emotional truth – that they can empathise better with a character trying *not* to show an emotion, than with one giving a gaudy display of bathos. As he says, a child trying not to cry is very moving, while a child bawling its eyes out is merely irritating. What the mask imposes upon the actor is restraint. This is because anything remotely 'showy' communicates itself as an untruth. This fact the Greeks knew well. The masks were unlikely to have been megaphones, and might have been only an aid to visibility. It has now been suggested that the masks were there in Greek theatre as a brake to overacting, to force the audience to feel and imagine the emotion, rather than an hysterical presentation of an emotion. The mask exposes the truth.

Masks of the sacred world

The subject of masks as cultural tools is a vast one, and there are many good books on the subject, precluding the need for me to repeat other people's research here. For a thorough exploration of the anthropo-logical aspects of the mask, John Mack's *Masks* (1994) is an excellent read. Suffice to say, many cultures, from European countries such as the United Kingdom, Germany, Switzerland and Austria, to the continents of Africa, Asia and the Americas, have a tradition of masked ceremonies which can still be seen today. North European traditions group around the marking of the banishment of winter and the arrival of spring, with the various fertility and harvest rites that go with it. Animals are often depicted, or scary beasts intent on frightening away the bad spirits. But these ceremonies are nowadays more about community and, sometimes, the tourist dollar, than about a real adherence to past pagan beliefs.

North American Indian masks are predominantly expressing spirits of the elements, to bring rain or sun for good harvests. Again, the huge variety of tribes means that there is a proportionally large variance in the uses for the mask. The more organised societies of Central and

Figures 2.1a and 2.1b Devil Ecuador [2.1a] and African mask [2.1b] from author's collection

South America have led to a clearer understanding of the role of the mask, in particular in the Aztec and Inca cultures. Many of these ancient masquerades, depicting spirits, elements, animals, have been adopted or subsumed by the imposed Christian beliefs of the conquering Spanish conquistadores of the sixteenth century. The Christian Devil is a mask often seen at South American festivals.

The African continent is home to a myriad of tribes and cultures, with as many masking traditions as there are languages. African societies used the mask, not only in the more orthodox way of representing the elements or spirits in hope of a good harvest, but also as ceremonial devices, used in dances and dramas, marking the important moments in peoples lives – births, deaths, coming-of-age, initiations and a host of other celebrations.

The dance and drama aspect of the mask is prevalent in the various cultures of Asia. Hindu ceremonies in India used performance as a way of telling the epic stories of the Gods, often in parades around the streets. Sri Lankan masks, like some in China, are 'curing' masks, and will drive out particular bad spirits that were thought to cause particular illnesses. The patient was placed at the centre of a circle of masked dancers, and the spirit of the sickness would leave when it saw the mask.

Finally, there is often a principal design difference between sacred and theatre masks. While the sacred mask exists as a vessel and its design influenced by totemic, religious and aesthetic criteria, most theatre masks rely on their attitude, the portrayal of character and emotion for their power.

Where our masks come from – the stock type

The theatre has its own rich tradition of mask use. Different cultures have followed different paths, so, to narrow it down and make it manageable, I have concentrated on the masks in western European theatre. When a mask enters the stage, it presents to the world an image of something fundamental about itself, its true attitude. This character comes to represent a certain kind of person within the society that would be recognisable to the audience. Sometimes this mask is called an archetype, showing traits seen in other characters across the centuries, coming to represent a universal truth about human character. Archetypes would include the fool, the hero, the trickster, the old crone and so on. A stereotype has less depth, mimicking less significant characters in the culture, or aping characteristics aligned to a person's profession. Finally, the stock type are the masks that seem to come down through the ages, which, when put together in different groupings form the basis for comic theatre. What is fascinating is that the stock types we see in our pantomimes at Christmas or at Punch and Judy shows on the beach have a history 3000 years old.

The first stock types appeared in Greece at the very beginning of what we would consider to be theatre itself. The early works of Greek drama, developing religious rituals (the dithyramb), were concerned with the stories of the Gods. The reasons why the Greeks performed in masks is naturally hazy, but the suggestions are that the combination of better acoustic properties, the ability to have one actor play several characters and stand out from the chorus, and better visibility for the audience meant that the mask quickly became synonymous, semantically, with the act of performing itself. And as previously stated, the emotional rigidity of the mask prevented overacting.

The first performances consisted of ritual choral dances, but theatre as we know it started to take shape when musical narration was added, allegedly by a man called Thespis – hence thespian. This new art arrived in Athens in 560 BC. The early Greek human masks of this time were fairly neutral in design, were worn like a helmet, and represented general types of character. These included 'King' or 'beardless youth'. Their demeanour was similar to that of Greek statues, where strong character features were replaced by a neutral and idealised facial expression, onto which the observer could project feelings and emotional narrative through the use of the actor's body language. To see this working now one has only to work in simple neutral masks, or think of the powerful pathos of Buster Keaton compared to the more clownic gurning of Charlie Chaplin.

The masks allowed the actors to play several characters, and to have their gestures seen at the back of the large amphitheatres. Originally there was only one definite actor onstage, apart from the chorus. This actor was often the poet, who spoke his own text. Aeschylus added another actor, as witnessed by the earliest surviving tragedies, and this then grew to three by the time of the *Oresteia* in 458 BC. Three actors but many roles. Why was this?

It has been suggested that there were few actors because the talent needed to work on the stage was a rare commodity. It has also been said that having such few actors allowed the audience to be able to work out who was speaking on stage – remember, these were big stages and vast amphitheatres. The plays were tightly choreographed, which precludes the idea that the actors were 'taken over' by the mask. If they were in a true trance state, how then could they follow such choreography? There seems to be a very short distance from the ritual use of the mask and the theatrical use, and one interesting point is this aspect of the actors' relationship between themselves and the mask. The earlier rituals saw the mask wearer becoming the mask, whatever it represented. By the sixth century the actors merely submerged themselves in the mask, before hurrying off to don another character. The description of an actor getting into character has resonances with the way we know Noh actors contemplate their masks, and Commedia dell'arte actors got into character. The Greek actors are said to have sat and studied their masks before a performance. Of course, once the show is up and running, one has merely time enough to throw the thing on and run onstage.

The basic character expressed by the Greek mask was developed on stage through action, through the making of decisions that set and sealed their fate. Though none survives today we know the masks were made of wood, cloth and cork, and the evidence of the Phylaxian and Dorian period suggest the emergence of stock types, emerging from the initial representation of Gods and then heroes. In the second century AD Julius Pollux wrote about the architecture and nature of the theatre, called the *Onomasticon*, including a documentation of the tragic and comic masks, with descriptions of features, colours and materials. Thespis was said to have experimented with different face coverings before adopting the traditional mask, and Aeschylus was the first to paint the mask. Pollux's categories were intended for tragedy only, with a few notes on the comedies.

- Six old men: smooth faced, white, grizzled, black haired, flaxen, and more flaxen.
- Seven young men: common, curled, more curled, graceful, horrid, pale, and less pale.
- Three slaves: leathern, peaked beard, flat nose.
- Ten women: hoary dishevelled, freed old woman, old domestic, middle aged, leathern, pale dishevelled, pale middle aged, shaven virgin, second shaven virgin, girl.
- There also existed 'specialist masks', which were pertinent to particular plays, representing actual or specific characters.

Greek theatre developed two principal strands, tragedy and comedy, represented by two masks, now seen as a shorthand for anything dramatic or theatrical. The comedies of Aristophanes were notable for the use of the chorus, becoming animal or fantastical, compared to the human chorus of the tragedies. These changes brought about new masks, and with the new masks came the possibility of parody, as the theatre moved further and further away from religious and moral subjects. The stock types used in Greek theatre expanded, and records were kept of their numbers. There existed about 30 in total in tragic theatre, and about 44 in the comedies. The great period of Greek drama came to an end around the tail of the fifth century BC, but masks continued to exert a great fascination over the popular culture of Greece and, later, Rome. The stock types that had now emerged were fairly neutral in character, relying for their definition on their looks rather than their attitude or temperament. With the development of Roman theatre, we start to see stock types emerging that are more recognisable, linking directly to the sixteenth-century Commedia dell'arte.

Figure 2.2 Greek acoustic female chorus masks by Mike Chase

The Roman theatre developed from the Greek model, but is considered a far inferior tradition. Comedy was more popular than tragedy, and the masks used were more caricatured and expressive. The religious and moral angle had gone, and the material was usually bawdy and licentious in execution. Considering that many plays appeared alongside the bloody combats at the gladiatorial games, it is difficult to see how the work could have been anything other than grotesque and over-the-top. The principal Roman playwrights were influenced by the theatre of the games, with stock characters appearing again and again, responding to their popularity.

The masks for the Roman theatre were not only cruder and clearer stock types, but also carried an enlarged forehead, known as the *onkos*. The two principal writers of the period were Plautus and Terence, and their work was based on the Greek comedies before them, but with particular Roman details. The servants were very important characters, a facet that carried on to the Commedia period. The Roman comedies eventually became the *mimus* and *pantomimus*, styles of knockabout farce with bawdy, vulgar dancing and singing. They were also known as the *atellanae*, short playlets that can be seen as direct precursors of the Commedia. Much of the comedy was derived from the lampooning of known characters from the area where they were being performed, with masks made to represent the characters. Certain stock types emerged which reappeared in the Commedia – the miser, the braggart, the fool and so on.

But the theatre of Rome became more and more lavish, until a revolt by writers such as Seneca, who wrote work to be read out loud, but not 'performed'. Theatre declined as Christianity flourished, all across Europe. By the sixth century all theatres had been closed.

The Dark Ages in Europe were not theatrically dead, but little remains to tell us about this period. The travelling troubadour, the *jongleur*, was popular, and the church started using drama to tell its stories to the illiterate populace. Mysteries, miracle plays and mummers all relied on the immediate audience recognition of the characters, with masks used to portray fantastical or devilish persona. Eventually, in Italy, the old Roman theatre re-emerged in a new form that still has influence today.

The Commedia dell'arte ('the professional comedy') is well served in John Rudlin's book *Commedia dell'arte: An Actor's Handbook* (1994). For a full history and description of this half mask based theatre form, look no further! As far as stock types were concerned, the Roman types re-emerged and new ones added: the miser, the braggart, the fool, the wily servant, the lovers, the pompous old man. Many of the *zanni*, the servant characters who often drove the stories, had animal characteristics. Arlechinno (Harlequin) is the most famous Commedia character, and appeared with dog or monkey-like attributes. The strength of Commedia, the reason behind its pan-European success, was the recognition factor. Audiences went to see known characters getting into scrapes and planning scams, with a liberal dose of specific

Figurte 2.3 Commedia Captain mask by Mike Chase

local allusion thrown in. A local duke might be portrayed for his penchant for young girls, or a notable bishop lampooned for girth and appetite. The reliance on stock types allowed the form to spread across Europe, with little variation in the mask style or costume. Colour might change, warts or hair were added, noses grew longer, but the essential attitude of each type remained the same. What was important was the plot and the comic business (lazzi) that each company developed for themselves.

Commedia started to die out in the late seventeenth century when playwrights started trying to tie the form down in set scripts, even dispensing with the masks. It lost its vivacity and was superseded by forms of theatre that were technically advanced and more psychological in depth. Naturalism and realism took over. As a historical form Commedia has inspired people ever since, in particular theatre-makers such as Gordon Craig, Vsevolod Meyerhold and Bertolt Brecht.

In the twentieth century the mask was used to explore the creative elements of the actor, the free-wheeling style inspired by the half mask prompting theatre-makers to look again at Commedia. Principal among these was Jacques Lecoq, a teacher in Paris whose school has influenced a whole generation of theatre-makers in the late twentieth century and early twenty-first century. He was the first in Europe to really explore the full mask as we know it today.

Lecoq's study of the mask came about initially, like many before him, through the rediscovery and exploration of Commedia. But after a while he started to experiment with the full mask, and was inspired by the masks seen at the Basle festival in Switzerland. This annual festival sees the town parading through the streets in a variety of masks that has its tradition back in pagan times. Mask-makers in the town produce white larval forms which are sold in shops and then decorated individually by the populace. Themes emerge each year, reflecting events in the town, region, or even the world. Lecoq took these unpainted masks and used them in his school, and a new style was created, the larval mask. Stock types emerged, like Commedia, as well as a broader range of types tailored to the work. The first company to use this style widely were the Moving Picture Mime Show, in their mask piece 'The Examination'.

Most mask theatre-makers of the late twentieth century have taken their inspiration from Lecoq, or from companies at one or two removes from him. Moving Picture Mime Show inspired the formation of Trestle Theatre Company, which in turn has spawned other companies. The American director Julie Taymor, an ex-student of Lecoq, has combined his ethos with her experiences living in Bali, to create a vibrant style that reached its peak – and a wide audience – with 'The Lion King'. This production has inspired a whole new generation of makers, designers and directors to explore the use of mask and puppet in performance.

Susan Harris Smith's book *Masks in Modern Drama* (1984) is an exhaustive study of the use of the mask in the twentieth century, albeit with a strong North American bias. It is worth exploring the

Figure 2.4 'The Examination', Moving Picture Mime Show

masks from the 1920s of W. T. Benda, or the ideas of Brecht and Eugene O'Neill, to realise that masks have been very well used in the twentieth century. Most of these uses have been the half mask, being a tool that writers found interesting to explore. The full mask has had less impact, possibly because of the absence of speech, rendering it more of an acquired taste, harder to write for, and limited in its application. The full mask has for centuries been a carnival tool, or an aid to ritual. As a silent expressive medium in itself it is relatively new.

What I find most fascinating about the mask is that, while many new forms of theatre are created from new, such as realism, naturalism, expressionism, theatre of cruelty, biomechanics, restoration, the musical, agit prop, dance drama, mask theatre clearly has its roots back in the earliest emergence of theatre itself. And while Commedia dell'arte can be seen as a significant watershed, even that influential form was a development of past ghosts treading the boards back in the mists of time.

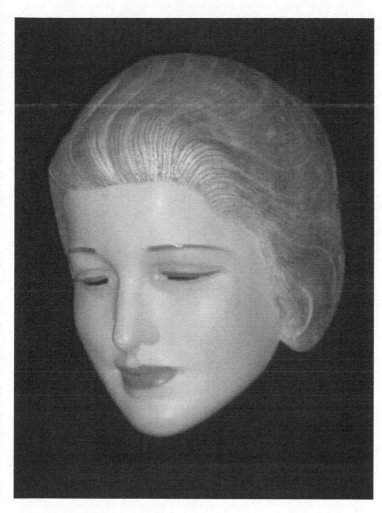

Figure 2.5 Mask of W. T. Benda. Collection of Larry Wood, Fantasy Guilde Studios.

CHAPTER 3

How the Mask Works

Many actors would baulk at the idea of using full masks on stage. Their principal means of expression has been taken away – the voice and the face. How then to communicate? Maybe they imagine a buffoon like mugging display, devoid of subtlety or substance. And yet the great actors of our time are used to working without the constant hum of text. Film actors have long recognised that a great deal of their innermost thoughts can be revealed through the minute changes in speed and rhythm that their bodies can portray. But on the stage, this visual, physical understanding is so often ignored. People seem terrified of silence. And yet our world is filled with sound that is not text. The sound of a knife placed on a table, a chair scraped back, the distant hum of traffic or an approaching storm – all atmospheric, dynamic colour that contributes to our understanding of an event. And then silence can be used for what it is, a powerful tool, a dramatic punctuation mark.

So not only have the usual media of expression been taken away, but also they have been replaced with a fixed face, a permanent expression that, surely, cannot change? But the beauty of mask work is the way that the audience perceive the mask to undergo many changes. It became a standing joke when I was touring with Trestle Theatre Company that at some point – virtually every night – a member of the audience would inquire about how we 'manipulated' the masks – how we got the expression to change. Because that is what they had per-ceived. What they were seeing in fact is one of the simplest but most effective tools of the full mask, the *countermask*. Countermask allows us to play virtually any emotion, playing contrary to the fixed expres-sion, purely by playing that emotion physically and truthfully. The audience's imagination does the rest. When the fixed attitude is allied with a clear character with a distinctive 'voice' – the unheard inner thought process – the sceptical actor will be amazed by how much can be communicated with the fixed face.

But we must acknowledge that the mask has its limits. It has rules and boundaries that can seem daunting. Jacques Lecoq called this the *via negativa*, a way of working in masks that confronts its limits and tries to find the positive things it can do, unlocking the creativity of performer and director to be as clever and communicative as possible despite the restrictions.

But how do the masks actually work ? Why can some people seem to bring the characters alive, showing great depth and substance to their work, and being completely believable, when others appear lumpen, clumsy and false?

The audience

The answer lies very close to what makes the live spectacle of theatre actually work. The first ingredient is the audience. It is their complicity in the process of a live event that brings meaning to the whole spec-tacle. Their suspension of disbelief must be total. They must wonder, as a child does, at the action in front of them. They must be willing to join in the game. When they see a masked actor on the stage, the audience need to become swiftly absorbed into the world that has been created. This need not be the real world, but a world real to itself. And the second part is the performer. In portraying their character, they need to be that person, rather than offering up an idea of the character. Their thought process must be true to that character. Here is how it works.

The human eye can focus on only a very small area at one time – about a centimetre. Everything around it is out of focus. Therefore the eye flickers about taking in small amounts of detail. An audience will always focus their attention on the face of the performer, and in detail they will try and focus on his or her eyes. But in a mask the human eye is not seen, so our brains readjust and take in a slightly larger area of interest – the whole face. This widening of focus therefore makes the brain more aware of the neck and torso, and it is this awareness that leads the audience to connect directly with the masked actor, since it is principally the relationship between the head and torso that expresses the most in mask theatre. Small readjustments of head, breath, suspensions in movement etc. all inform the audience of the character's innermost thoughts, as if the way that we carry our heads – the centre of our intelligence and very being – is beyond falsehood. The gimbal that is the neck joint, with its myriad of possible positions, enables the head–torso relationship to have a vast vocabulary at its disposal, in relation to the speed and rhythm of its movement, and in its spatial positioning.

In a nutshell . . .

Lecoq explained it brilliantly. The mask displaces the principal communication methods. So in a mask the whole face becomes the eye, the part that sees things, and the body becomes the expressive face, which registers the realisations. Think about that for a moment. Instead of the eye flicking about, seeing things, and the face registering in response to what the eye sees, now the whole head must move to see. This helps pinpoint the audience's attention, helps them see that which the mask sees. The body then reacts to what it has seen, not in any overblown fashion, but a simple change in tension, breath, alignment, done organically and without artifice. This is the truest and simplest explanation for how the mask works.

To explore the incredibly simple but powerful relationship between head and torso, use neutral masks, or colanders, or a bucket! Put a paper bag over the head! Simply transform the human face into a different state by masking, and then play around with simple movements that suggest sadness, joy, an idea, realisation, negative and affirmative responses. Speed and rhythm changes will speak volumes with the smallest amount of movement.

The inner monologue

The actor's actions on stage are underpinned by a continuous thought process, a running commentary in the voice of the character. This unheard commentary underlines their movement, which offers up clarity to the observer. Audiences read the movement by adding their own commentary, filling in the thought process with their own words, a process which silently and often subconsciously chugs along nonstop. So they are listening to their own voice, their own vocabulary, based on their own experience of life. Therefore it becomes very personal to each individual member of an audience. It also means that the work can play to a broad range of people, with differing experiences of theatre, of different languages and cultures. While words can be very illuminating, they can also be alienating, a barrier between playwright and audience. Masks let the audience experience a character's emotions and thoughts almost first hand, involving them deeply in the spectacle. But when audiences commit like this, so the opportunity for letting them down increases.

The problems start when the actor starts 'acting', rather than 'being'. The relationship between movement and thought process is a delicate one, and relies on the actor's clear and economic use of movement. Extraneous gestures, or doing action that has no truth behind it, will make the audience aware of the actor behind the mask, breaking an illusion which they believe to be real. This is the worst offence imaginable! If the audience are aware of the actor, or of the pretence of it all, then the performer has failed. An audience will become immediately aware of the falsehood if the actor uses movement or gesture not underpinned by thought. This is because it is the actor's thoughts that the audience are interpreting in their own heads. No thought, no truth! An interesting exercise to do in the latter stages of

Figure 3.1 Crèche, Trestle Theatre Company, Sally Cook as the little girl

rehearsal is to remove the mask from the performers, and get them to run through the work, talking their internal monologue out loud. It swiftly becomes apparent when the actor doesn't know what he or she is supposed to be thinking. And if they don't know, the audience don't stand a chance of knowing!

The actor

So how then do we portray character so completely and convincingly? Many people suppose that a mask actor must enter a trance for it to work properly. I reject this idea. The place for the trance state is in psychodrama or drama therapy, or in the studio. It has no place on the stage. A mask can portray the subtle or hidden nuances of a character's inner life only when the performer is in control. This doesn't mean the actor can't get 'lost' in the character or the action. In this respect, masked acting is no different from unmasked acting. Performers can be totally immersed, and yet have one small part of their consciousness aware of the mechanics of what they are doing – because they are going to have to do it again tomorrow night. And because to be clear about what you are saying in the mask takes a degree of skill, and no small amount of choreography.

To understand the thought process further, let me describe it to you visually. A character's actions often speak for themselves. If they are making tea we understand the action, though we might be unaware of their feelings, their attitude to making the tea or something else entirely. The speed and rhythm with which they move gives us some idea of their character, and their general attitude. But we don't walk about constantly emoting. When the character feels something specific, or comments personally on something, it is like opening up the face of a clock and momentarily seeing the cogs turning. The actor has a phrase in his or her head that can be shown through a slight gesture, or a movement of the torso, an intake of breath. This can be directed straight to the audience, if this convention of 'clocking the audience' is to be used, or it can done for their own benefit. Once it has finished, the clock face closes up and the action continues.

The physical phrase

The verbal phrase has a natural length, and therefore so does the physical phrase. Over- or underplaying the length of this phrase will come across as a falsehood. Put simply, if a character were to ask another if they would like a drink, the gesture they use must last as long as it takes for that character to say 'Would you like a drink?' The tendency is for the actor not to trust the mask or the audience and instead overplay the gesture, resulting in a confused message to the audience, along the lines of 'Would you like like a drink drink drink would you would you?' In the mask, an actor must find the truth behind a gesture or comment, and play it for its compatible length.

This skill involved in understanding the length and weight of gesture is the skill of an animal – the human animal – needed to relate to the world around us. It is the skill that enables us to understand other people's social skills, and ultimately, whether or not they are a threat to us. As such, it is a subconscious skill, something innate and organic, which makes our understanding of masks personal, powerful and yet curiously indefinable! When Dr. Mehrabian declared that 56 per cent of the impact of communication is through body language, it is precisely through this simple understanding and playing of gesture that the bulk of communication happens.

So at the heart of good mask work is the audience's belief in the transformation, of actor into character. In this respect, it is no different from unmasked theatre. But a mask actor doesn't have a script to work from, instead relying on an improvisation technique to create the work. A writer may structure the work, but it is the actor who must fill the minutes, seconds and nano-seconds of a character's life on-stage. It is very much theatre of the actor, since he or she has a high level of responsibility to what happens onstage. All actors create their character's movement, but a mask actor must also create the logic, the continual inner life. And he or she must then work out how to get that across.

Realisation, decision, action

The body becomes the principal tool of expression, Lecoq's 'face'. This does not mean that performers need to be experts in illusionary mime, or dance trained. It simply means that they must be able to put across what they are thinking using only the speed and rhythm of their movement. Once they have established how the character moves, (its rhythm, its walking pace, its sitting and standing mode), actors can move on to finding the interruptions to these movements. From this they can develop the reaction speeds of the character, the working cogs that show us their realisations, their decision-making and then their response, carried on into action. Imagine a character, an old woman. She walks into a room, and is about to sit down. Halfway seated she hears a noise outside. She freezes, thinks, *realises* what the sound means, *decides* what to do, and *acts*, maybe by standing and fearfully going to the window. This seemingly pedantic sequence has a clear thought process, which translates itself to the audience, who can feel her disquiet. And it is through the manipulation of objects around us that we can signify the inner workings of the mind. While she may walk directly to the window, it is her hands that play nervously with the brooch on her cardigan that tells us she is ill at ease. It is this concentration on the minutiae, rather than the expansive gesture and overplayed character walk, which gives the mask its authority and truthfulness. And it is the expansion of the moments of thought, and the willingness to communicate them to an audience, that makes the mask speak volumes (see the exercises in Chapter 6).

Less is more

It quickly becomes apparent when working in masks that a simple though dogmatic edict may be that '*less is more*'. Stillness coming out from movement can be enormously powerful, as though underlining the movement with a red pen. It is as if the thought itself is in inverted commas, standing slightly apart from the rest of the movement. It alerts the audience to something significant, such as portraying an important thought or reaction. This stillness, however fleeting, before and after a 'cogs working' moment brings clarity and thus understanding. It is an oft-repeated mistake of novice mask-users that their first entrance is accompanied by a flailing of arms and a twitching head. A simple command to stop, or maybe asking them to hold onto a fixed object such as the wall, can bring the character into a more productive state. This must be accompanied by an understanding of tension (Chapter 5), and how that inner tension manifests itself. A psychopath may enter the stage and seem perfectly normal. How then can you portray the inner turmoil of their mind?

Remember Sir Peter Hall's comment. It is more intriguing seeing a character trying *not* to express an emotion than one constantly demanding our attention. The silent child with the trembling lip is more interesting to us than the bawling one. These moments of emotional self-confrontation in a mask are without doubt the most powerful.

Finally, it is no good the actors having a wonderful inner monologue if they are unable to put it across to an audience convincingly. They must be able to tell us about it, constantly. They must tell us how they feel. That after all is what we are interested in. The actor is doing it (we hope) for us! So tell us! Telling the audience everything happens in two ways. First, the mask observes the fourth wall, but seems to be undertaking a constant conversation with itself, full of the nuances of actual speech but actioned through simple gesture, shrugs, nods, changes in speed and rhythm etc. The second way is for all the above to happen, but the mask also stops and tells the audience directly, at a specific point, what it is thinking. This is usually a realisation or a decision point, and uses the audience like a TV camera. For example, a character walks on stage, and trips over. The character looks back at the floor, tutting, then sees the audience, and tuts to them directly. It's a constant flow of thought to the audience, allowing them to hear the voice of the mask in their own head. This is called 'clocking' the audience and again, most important, is that the gesture to the audience follows the verbal/physical phrase rules mentioned previously.

Masks and film

Not masks on film, but it is interesting to note how producing work for masks is similar to creating film. The greatest mask director, Julie Taymor, spent her formative years in Paris watching movies. I am often asked who my influences are, and I think people are surprised when I reel off the names of film directors such as Akira Kurosawa, David Lynch, Stanley Kubrick, David Lean, Joel and Ethan Coen, Jean-Pierre Jeunet and Tim Burton, instead of a list of theatre directors. Which is not to say that I'd rather be making film. No, I love theatre, the magic of the game that can never exist in a cinema. But for me the allure of film is about the construction of the visual narrative, the ability to explode or expand moments, and the way the soundtrack and music is as much a part of the emotional journey.

My favourite exercise at college was to spend an hour or so travelling from our suburban base into central London on the tube or bus, imagining that my eye was a camera. One starts to frame shots. You see life differently, become acutely aware of special relationships between people and their environment. Small everyday happenings become imbued with a weight and a magic that is marvellous to observe, as though through a lens. It is as if life is one vast movie set for one's own edification. Directing masks has a similar feel, voyeuristically watching a character in its unseen moments, being privy to private thoughts. I have often thought how close mask acting is to screen acting, and so I was delighted when I came across this snippet about Dirk Bogarde, as seen by his co-star Charlotte Rampling.

'He's one of the actors who gets closest to making it possible for the spectator to actually feel that they are *inside* his thoughts and know what he's thinking. It's about silence and it's about allowing the camera to invade you. It's a magnetic quality. You are compelled to look, and the more you look, the more you're drawn into that person.'

For me, that brilliantly describes acting in a mask.

CHAPTER 4

Applications

So why use full masks in the first place? There are two approaches. Either you decide to do a full mask production, to explore their use and to work to their strengths, or you decide to use masks after a certain amount of production planning has been done, to fulfil a particular need.

Whichever approach you use, the question 'Why use masks?' should always be asked. What am I adding by using masks? Wouldn't it be better without? Is the idea the best vehicle for masks? Let's first look at what the use of full masks can bring to a production.

The full mask has the facility to concentrate the audience's attention on the inner life of a character, in a different way from that seen through the use of text. It is more open to audience interpretation, allowing for a broader experience, less confined by the rigid meaning of words. Masks can highlight the physical relationship between people, and the way aspects of a relationship, often the unsaid and subconscious, manifest themselves physically. There are many practical benefits with masks. A small cast can play many characters convincingly, crossing the age and sex barriers without the audience being aware of the number of performers involved. Mixing masked and unmasked actors can be used to delineate clearly between reality and fantasy, present and flashback, or between different worlds. Their highly visual nature makes them ideal for use in street theatre, when it is impossible to be heard above the noise of the traffic.

Perhaps the biggest advantage of using masks is the matter of recognition, a factor well understood by the travelling Commedia dell'arte troupes of the sixteenth century. By using a visual stereotype – a grumpy old man, a gormless punk, a bullying child – you let the audience make quick judgements about the characters, to recognise their fundamental 'type'. This can allow you to get on with the action, observation or narrative straight away, and possibly confound the audience's expectations of the characters, thus breaking the stereotype. Commedia used clear social types that were understood no matter which region of Italy or France they were playing in. This enabled them to develop their scanty plot lines quickly, indulging in knockabout antics and using local knowledge to appeal to its specific audience. So a local lord might come in for some improvised stick during a servant's rant about the injustices of his master. An audience seeing a full mask show can often be heard commenting on the similarity between characters on stage, and various members of their own families!

At their best, masks are about people, and their relationships with those around them. Whether working through a strong narrative, or through observation, they can produce powerfully emotive theatre that involves the audience uniquely in the process, allowing you to tackle difficult themes by focusing on what they mean to a handful of characters. You can present a situation as action, letting the audience provide the moral judgements, or raise the questions that are pertinent to them personally. It can seem that the audience is like a hidden spy camera, clandestinely watching an event unfold. There are no soliloquies, no theories propounded, no answers. There are just actions, reactions and emotions.

Observation

The simplest form of full mask production is the observation piece. This concentrates on a bunch of characters in one or two recognisable situations, and is created largely through improvisation. The masks are very much in control, as the piece is structured around the relationships between people in different groupings. Plot can be thin or totally absent. One of the first full mask observation pieces seen in modern theatre was 'The Examination' by the Moving Picture Mime Show (1977) (p. 2, 25). This Lecoq-trained trio used large Basle style masks to show several boys and their teacher before, during and after a school exam. The characters were clearly defined – the swot, the thickie, the nerd – and the piece consisted simply of these characters interacting in the situation. They had obvious objectives, which invariably clashed with each other, thus creating drama, and though a comedy, its emotional finale showed the simple power latent in the large larval masks, when coupled with a disciplined acting style.

Different time/space continuum!

But the full mask is not limited to playing within its own world. As a dramatic tool, masks can be used in many different ways. Lou Stein's production of *The Picture of Dorian Gray* at Watford Palace theatre used a full mask to depict the aged Dorian Gray in the final moments of the play. The joint Trestle/Millstream theatre co-production of *House of Straw* (1995) used mask characters to depict the ghosts that inhabited a house recently acquired by the protagonist, who, with his wife and next-door neighbour, were unmasked. It is not easy mixing the styles. The focus of a mask is much stronger than an unmasked actor. The thinking times are very different – it is easy for an unmasked actor to make a mask look like a difficult child – and it is easier generally for an actor using text to get across plot points. An audience must work when a mask is on stage, which may account for much of the satisfaction they derive from a mask show.

Fantasy versus reality

It is most important that you are clear in your own mind why you are using masks in a mixed production. It can be very simple – to portray something fantastical, or to show flashback – and in Trestle's production of *Top Storey* (1987) we reversed the expectation, and used masks to show both the present and past, through observation, and then used speaking actors to act out fantasy stories being read from a comic by one of the mask characters. The reason may be more obtuse, being concerned with the nature of communication, or the lack of it. *Ties that Bind* (1989) had a main character, unmasked, who could not communicate with those around her, and they were portrayed as masks. Only her teacher, with whom she had an affinity, was unmasked with her, creating an opportunity for dialogue. This possibility, in a bleak piece about incest and abuse in the home, acted as a safety valve, with the audience hoping that if things got too bad, she could always talk to her teacher.

Street theatre

The mask's imposing and eye-catching physical presence, plus their silence makes them extremely useful as tools for street theatre. Commedia was at its heart a street art form, and relied on music, whistles and singing to drum up an audience – but they didn't have to contend with the noise of modern traffic. One of the hardest aspects of attracting and holding an audience for street theatre is the other pressures for their attention. Getting a crowd to become absorbed in a drama amidst the hustle and bustle of a modern town can be very hard, so the intense focus and silence of a full mask is a great boon. The downside is that sometimes it is hard to maintain the magic, due to the proximity to the crowd and the attentions of small children.

My initial mask experiences were spent creating work for the street, a great learning process about what makes an audience want to watch you. There are increasingly more and more companies dedicated to the street arts, from the United States, Australia, New Zealand and the

Figure 4.1 Flowerpots, **Natural Theatre Company**

United Kingdom. In particular, the Spanish have developed work that is anarchic, vibrant and very exciting. Many of these companies use the mask or the puppet as a principal tool of expression. Early 1970s companies such as the San Francisco Mime Troupe or Bread and Puppet Theatre Company (both from the United States) used the highly visual media of the mask and puppet to make compelling political theatre that existed outside of the normal and established forum for theatre.

The real power behind using masks on the street is the obvious clash between two completely realised real worlds. The world of the mask, created as an antidote or mirror to the real world, finds itself at the heart of its antithesis. Passers-by cannot help but stop and stare.

Masks and illusion

The mask has often been associated with the art of illusionary mime, and is often a companion subject at colleges and mime schools. So it follows that at some point people will try to combine the two skills.

Moving Picture Mime Show would present double bills, with a mask play following a piece of pantomime blanche. But they never, to my recollection, combined the two forms in one piece. This is because a mask character *can't do mime*! Maybe it's me being a bit dogmatic about it, but illusionary mime requires actors to be able to focus on the objects and environment they are creating, and for the audience to be aware of that focus. A mask can't do this, since with most full masks the actor's eyes aren't visible. Therefore the idea doesn't really work; it's one convention too many. Try it for yourself and decide.

Conventions

Of course, masks are capable of carrying a strong narrative – you just have to discover what you want to tell, and how you are going to tell it, realising your limitations and working within boundaries. But no matter what form the work takes, several benefits of masks are immediately apparent.

- Multi-roles – many characters, few actors.
- Cross-dressing – boys become women, girls become men.
- Cross-ageing – a good actor should be able to portray any age in a mask, from infant to great age.

It is said that Roscius, one of the earliest mask actors in Rome, took up the mask because he wanted to act but had a terrible voice. There are many reasons for donning the mask, for deciding to use them in a production. Whichever one it is, recognise it bravely, and stick to the conventions you have decided upon, and half the battle is done!

As a convention, the mask can offer up many problems – in essence, Lecoq's *via negativa* mentioned earlier. But they also offer an intensity of experience that outweighs the practical stumbling blocks. And so long as the thought behind the convention is crystal clear, masks as a tool can be used in any live performance medium.

CHAPTER 5

Preparing for the Mask

The mask is a tool of theatre. It should be respected but not revered. There is no magic latent in itself, but when used properly can generate enormous power that directly influences the audience's imagination. And like a power tool, it requires just the right amount of power to make it work. Too much or too little and the tool will not function properly. Too much power may manifest itself in exaggerated gestures, excess fidgeting and an inability to *stop moving*! Too little power will fail to animate the body sufficiently to communicate effectively. Either way, if the tool is not powered up correctly, it will fail to live in the audience's imagination, and they will quickly tire of its superficiality.

Initial exercises

The objective of the first encounters with the mask is simply to bring the character alive, to make it real in front of an audience – even an audience of one. There is no point in trying or rehearsing mask work without someone sitting out front to accept the transformation, and to give feedback as to its effectiveness. If you are not used to it, wearing a mask the first few times can seem really weird – it's hard to see, difficult to breathe, and it's easy to feel curiously detached. But stick with it. Concentrate on listening to the inner voice of the character, the thought process that ticks away the entire time you are on stage.

To prepare yourself or the group for putting on masks, I suggest you undertake some preliminary work. This involves getting used to portraying thoughts, emotions and character through simple body language, as well as understanding the restraints put upon you by the mask – principally that the mask needs to be played 'out' to the audience as much as possible.

One vital point. The learning that takes place in many of the exercises both here and in the next chapter is not confined to the participant. There is much to be gleaned from observing the work, so question the audience about how they felt about the exercise. What worked and what didn't? Why did something not work? What was the best bit, and why? Very few of the exercises involve the whole group, particularly when we get to put the masks on, so make people aware that the process of learning about masks is as much about observing as it is about doing.

If you feel that the students are sceptical about the mask, here is a very quick taster to whet their appetite, which also reinforces the above point. In front of an audience, place five to ten people with their backs to the audience, no less than eight feet from them. Get the actors to don a mask each, sorting out hair and elastic etc. Standing, ask them to turn around, but to do nothing. Then ask them to slowly drop their heads to their chest. Then ask them to quickly look up to the audience. Then slowly up to the sky, snap back to the audience etc. It can be seen immediately how effective the simple movements and different rhythms are for the audience, and should excite them about how much more can be achieved when the actor can actually move at will. Repeat the exercise with different students, to allow the first batch to see the masks working.

EXERCISE: CROSSING THE ROOM

Mind-bogglingly easy. Ask the students to cross from one side of a room to another, but always playing the face to the front, as if to an audience. Ask them to turn at some time on their journey, and make sure they understand that the correct turn would see them *not* turning their backs on the audience.

Hold a mask up, and ask them to pull the face of the mask on their own face. How does that make them feel? Get them to find a walk that suits the face, finding a speed and rhythm of movement that creates a simple sense of character. Then repeat the 'Crossing the room' exercise.

Cutting out the turns, instead give them a simple action halfway across the room that would elicit a contrary emotion, the *countermask* effect that is so important. For example, show them a grumpy mask. Ask them to cross the room as that character, pulling that face. Halfway across they find a £50 note. How can they show their elation physically without changing the face, *and* keeping in character?

Happy masks step in puddles, angry masks find dead pets etc. This starts them thinking about *countermask*.

EXERCISE: CENTRES OF PERSONALITY

A fun character exercise. Imagine that the centre of your personality is located in a different part of the body. How does this affect your speed and rhythm of movement? It doesn't necessarily mean leading with that part of the body, but finding a walk where it seems to be imbued with some importance. It could be the chin, the left knee, the stomach, the feet or hands, the forehead or nose. An advanced notion would to be to place the centre outside the body, such as behind or in front of the head, *under* the feet, between the legs! How subtle or exaggerated can they become?

Since most of the initial work in masks is improvised, some younger students and even some actors may require some impro practice, to open them up to possibilities, and for them to realise the pointlessness of 'blocking'. The idea of '*No*' should not occur to them in a mask at first. If you say to a mask during a hot-seat exercise 'I hear it's your birthday', they can't indicate that it's not – since it limits the journey that they may travel, and may cause the workshop leader to run out of ideas! Here are a couple of old favourites.

EXERCISE: YES, AND . . .

Two people have a conversation, each line starting with the words 'Yes, and . . .' The impro should build in terms of tension and silliness.

'Shall we go on holiday together?'
'Yes, and you could bring your mother.'
'Yes, and we could bury her in the sand.'
'Yes, and leave her there when the tide comes in.'
'Yes, and then the crabs could argue over who eats what.'
'Yes, and . . .' etc.

It's about accepting what other people give you, and developing it – a principal impro skill.

EXERCISE: PRESENTS

Start by giving a partner an imaginary box, of any size. Don't say what is in it – because you don't know. Let the person unwrap and say what it is – 'Wow, thank you, a model of the Eiffel Tower'. Discuss the present briefly, then let the other person respond by giving you a present. Then open it and say what it is etc.

Next, give the partner a present, but state what it is: an emotion – fear, jealousy, greed, love, happiness, paranoia. For fun, have the present inside an incongruous package, e.g. 'I'd like to give you this thimble full of . . . rage'. The partner now takes the thimble and responds in the given emotion – rage. The donor provokes the partner, and they have a short interchange.

'Why did you give me this, I hate it!'
'I saw it and thought of you.'
'How dare you insult me like that!'
'Aren't you over-reacting a bit?'
'No I'm bloody not, you idiot . . .' etc.

After a short while the impro stops, the recipient gives back a different package containing a different emotion, and the exercise is repeated.

Then try this exercise in a circle, the package being passed from one person to the next, so in effect they are doing it for an audience. Why do we like some people's responses more than others? What we enjoy most is:

* truth
* immediacy
* lack of inhibition
* surprise.

Gesture lines

When gestures are placed at certain levels of the body they carry with them subliminal meanings. In real life we don't think about these lines but they happen anyway, part of our natural body language that happens without us thinking about it when we speak. If you have a text, then the gestures happen automatically, though one of the ways we perceive bad acting is when the gesture doesn't fit the line. With mask acting when there is no audible text we need to have an understanding of how gestures work, and one of these is the 'gesture line'.

- Gestures that happen below the waist are usually offhand gestures, not important as they are far away from the centre of intellect, the brain. But if these gestures are strong gestures then they become very earthy and animalistic – very sexual.
- Gestures from the stomach area are truthful gestures – the gut reaction. They are warm and embracing, soft and motherly. But if you harden them up they become desperate for the truth, with a yearning or desperate quality.
- Gestures from the chest are heartfelt and personal, pleading, often emotional.
- Gestures from the face are sensual and sensuous, immediate and tactile. Think of the Italian gesture from the mouth.
- Gestures from above the eyes to above the head are mad, wild, uncomprehending or exasperated. They are often jubilant or tragic.

EXERCISE: GESTURES

Have several actors stand on stage and face an audience. Give them a simple line that can be said in a variety of ways such as 'Will you come home?' or 'You didn't mean that!' Have them say the line to the audience simultaneously, with an accompanying gesture from a particular part of the body, repeating it several times to try out different ways of doing it. See what effect the gesture has upon the line. Try singly with variations. Discuss with the audience the meaning of the gesture.

Tension and energy

Since we are dealing primarily with physical expression, it is useful to have a clear understanding of how tension and energy effect what we are saying and how we are saying it. There are two kinds of body language involved, that I shall call *mono* and *stereo*.

Mono is when the physical tension is clearly matched by the intention. To put it another way, the body energy is in sync with the brain's energy. For example, a man rushes into the room and screams 'FIRE!' and proceeds to rush about, yelling at people to leave. People pick up the clear signal, an unambiguous message that there is a fire in the building and it is time for them to leave. Other thoughts he may be having are not expressed – for instance, his wife might have left him that morning!

But supposing that man, on discovering the fire, had wet himself. He now has to run about the building, from room to room, warning people about the impending conflagration, with a large wet patch down his trousers. This is no doubt going to affect his performance – he will be giving a more ambiguous message, and some people may become preoccupied with his state of mind. This is because he is now in *stereo*. The energy of his body is at odds with that of his brain. He wants to tell people that there is a fire and that they must leave, but he doesn't want to draw attention to himself!

Being in *stereo* is not necessarily a negative thing. A young man is crazy about a woman. His mind is afire with passion and strategies for seducing her. But he is playing it cool, very relaxed and mature. He is driving towards what he really wants, while appearing to be not that fussed. Very compelling!

There exists something called *the seven states of tension*, whose origins I can never quite pin down, though I suspect they come from Lecoq. They are well known among some theatre directors as a very useful tool for directing actors in relation to the energy of scenes and relationships. The states are in effect a ladder of tension in the body, each rung given a number and a name, with the tension increasing with each step up the ladder. It is important to note that these states are about pure tension and energy, and nothing at all to do with character or emotion. For instance, the state of number five – quite high up the ladder, could be applied to a love scene as well as a fight, somebody cooking or someone shouting 'Fire!'

The application of the seven states to masks is of great value, as well as applying them to other areas such as chorus work. Think of them as 'acting by numbers'. All the participants need to be aware of the language, so the director can say 'Try that again, but in four', and everyone knows what he or she means.

The states can be used to provoke devising – a character goes into a room in one state and emerges in another. What happened? For the mask, the tension with which a character communicates has great import, so getting it right, or manipulating it to increase effectiveness, is very useful. It creates a language that is divorced from emotion, allowing the performer to make their own adjustments while responding to comments from the outside.

So here they are. Origin unknown, and no doubt altered from an original. Each state has a name and a number.

EXERCISE: THE SEVEN STATES OF TENSION

One   Exhaustion

The first rung, and a physical state almost entirely devoid of tension – just enough to stand upright. Not very exciting, but you have to start somewhere. Everything is imbued with an extreme lethargy, the brain can't function properly and nothing can be really achieved. Every muscle is fatigued, there seems to be an ongoing battle between you and gravity. Any less tension and gravity would win. But mix it in stereo with another state and you have an interesting dichotomy. For example, a character is asleep, obviously in 'one'. But the character is having a nightmare, being chased by six-foot rabbits, so state 'six' is also present. Maybe the character's legs and eyelids are twitching, and the person is whimpering. But on its own, number one isn't very dramatic.

Two   The Californian

This is the state of being relaxed, very fluid, cool and mercurial. The body never quite settles, and it has the feeling of the non-committal about it. This lends itself to a sense of danger with this state, since you can never be sure what it is thinking. Again, this state mixes well with an internal state from higher up the ladder. Physically the state is very hip-centric, with the non-committal idea physicalised into a swaying hip that never settles.

Three   The stage manager

The hardest state to achieve, the state of neutrality – see the neutral mask in Chapter 11. It is called the stage manager, since that person is trying to appear invisible, if needed on stage. The tension with which they move is devoid of anything other than the task at hand. There is no emotion, no future or past focus, just the right energy to do the job. Observing someone working in 'three' is to watch someone giving nothing away. This state may seem uncaring, disinterested, clinical. But mix it with the idea that the most emotional thing is to see someone trying not to give way to an emotion, and you have a useful and simple device for finding a sense of truth in the playing of a scene.

Four   The director

The state of being interested and critical, always looking for the best. Physically, this state may be head led, the body following what the eye sees. There is a keen sense of urgency and commitment here, people following what is most important to them. This state is very useful for a chorus, where the energy can often become moribund. The desire to move forward is palpable, with the intentions and energy being very outward. This state expresses enthusiasm for something – anything, actually, from 'I want you', to 'I want you dead'! Sometimes this is called the 'forward' state because gestures and intent are all in front of the character.

Five   Is there a bomb in the room?

This question is loaded with *possibility*, and therefore this is the state of the optimist, a sort of number four with knobs on. The tension is really palpable now, unambiguous, and everything is very forward, with a compelling urgency. 'Is there a bomb in the room?' could be played as a tempestuous love scene, a fight to the death or a chorus telling an audience about a sea voyage. The sense of the possible, the optimistic makes it a very positive state even when communicating something negative. Gestures are wider and wilder, but still in front of the body.

Six   There is a bomb in the room!

The tension has been screwed up even higher, and the sense goes from something being possible, to becoming *probable*. This makes it a pessimistic state, a state that suggests a sense of phobia about something. It has become overwhelming. 'I love you so much I can't speak!' The statement suggests that there is too much information to take in, too much to do, which means that none of it will ever really be achieved – hence the sense of being overwhelmed. Physically, it has the idea of not being able to think straight because the thoughts cannot be put into a recognisable order. The brain is being bombarded with conflicting and overwhelming information. The tension is so high in this state that you cannot reason with a character like this. Gestures have started to move above the head.

Seven   The bomb has gone off

The state of total tension, or rigor mortis, a singular freezing up of all the muscles and sinews in the body at the realisation that what was about to happen has just happened. Clearly, whatever it is matters, otherwise there wouldn't be this much tension. It might be a character reacting to missing their train, seeing their team score a goal, smashing a cup in frustration, slamming the telephone down. It is often seen as a release of tension, so that the character then reverts to a different state once the safety valve of seven has blown.

Exercises for the tension states

Once the states have been learnt, it is useful to start applying them so that students can begin to feel them for themselves. Initially we give them structure to work around, so they can concentrate on their physicality.

EXERCISE: THE ART GALLERY

A useful scenario is the art gallery. Imagine a character or characters passing time looking at pictures on the wall. They can talk to each other – this is not in masks – and find the state's vocal qualities. In one they just shuffle around the room. In two, they are looking at the pictures in a disinterested or smarmy way. In three they are just looking at the pictures because they have to. In four they are looking for a particular picture. In five they want to find that picture but the gallery shuts in two minutes – and if they can find this priceless painting, it's theirs! In six they have only 30 seconds to find the picture, and there are too many to look at. They're losing the picture! In seven the announcement is made closing the gallery. The priceless picture is lost.

EXERCISE: THE STATION

Another scenario is to talk a group of students through from one to seven, and down again, when they are on a railway station. You can elaborate on this simple format.

1 Early morning, going to work, half-asleep on the platform.
2 Starting to wake up, stroll about, no worries about the day ahead. Greeting fellow travellers etc.

3   You do this so often you switch off. The train should be here in a minute, so you're just . . . waiting.

4   The train is due now. Agitation increases as watches and timetables are checked, and necks crane towards the direction of the expected train.

5   The train is late. You have an important job interview to get to. Although it doesn't make the train come, you have to stride about, or fidget nervously.

6   The train is too late to make your connection. Even if it comes now, you will have missed the interview. You are overwhelmed with powerless frustration.

7   'The 7:35 to East Croydon has been cancelled.' Aaaarrrgghhh!

If you have two groups you can swap over at this point.

7   After the interview, for which you were very late. You slam the door behind you as you leave the room. Aaaarrrgghhh! You blew it.

6   Aware that the entire office is looking at you, you make your way in a highly paranoid state through the office and out of the building.

5   Outside, you realise that if you hurry, you can get the early train home. You hurry through the streets.

4   At the station, you look up at the platform indicator and quickly seek out your platform.

3   Knowing you have time, you walk calmly to your platform to find the train standing there waiting for you.

2   Glad now to be on your way home, relaxed, you amble through the carriage to find the best seat.

1   Exhausted, you slump into the seat and fall fast asleep.

EXERCISE: THE HOLY GRAIL

A simpler exercise would be to place all the students at one end of the room and have them travel the length of the space, going from one to seven over the course of the journey. At the far end is the holy grail, that which they've striven for all their life. They have to justify the change from five into six, and then, inches from their lifelong goal, they hit seven!

Developing the states

A character, once established, can play its own version of every state. Once you have established this basic vocabulary, there are lots of games and exercises you can invent, to encourage students to work physically. Once the mask has been introduced and become comfortable, the tension states are applicable when devising and directing.

EXERCISE: MONO AND STEREO STATES

As an impro exercise, set up simple scenes of conversations, giving the participants an inner and an outer tension state, with a clear logic. For example;

- A boy is trying to be cool and finish with his girlfriend (a two on the outside), but he knows the last train home is in five minutes (his brain is in five). She wants to throw herself at him (a five inside), but she is allergic to his aftershave (a six outside).
- Two people are talking about holidays, very excited in five. One person suddenly remembers that the last time they went away

together, they argued all the time, and adds a cool two inside. The other one remembers that she's left the gas on at home, but doesn't want to look stupid (a seven inside).

You can make up a plethora of exercises using the seven states. Get the students to place characters in a simple situation, such as a prison cell, doctor's surgery etc., and have characters coming and going, in clear states, changing states, mixing states, responding to events and people around them.

Speed and rhythm

There is, of course, a much simpler way of exploring tension and energy. Give the students an emotion such as fear. Ask them to simply walk about, or engage in a simple task. Then, using a scale of 1–6, ask them to show their fear through the speed and rhythm of their movement. At level 1, it is very secretive, hardly perceptible, at level 2 we see that something is troubling them, and at level 3 it is clear that the character is scared. Beyond that we enter the realms of overacting, but it's a useful exercise to acknowledge that which I have already stated, which is that it is more dramatic and intriguing watching a character trying to suppress an emotion that watching them give full vent to it.

Now develop the idea. This time you gradate the level of fear, as well as the amount that it is portrayed. So they can *feel* fear on a 1–6 scale, and *show* fear on a 1–6. For instance, they are walking home at night. They are terrified that they are being followed – a level 5 of fear, but they are trying not to show that anything is upsetting them – a level of 1. They get to a police station and can't get served. They exaggerate their show of fear – up to a level 3, but they feel safer now, so the feeling of fear is down to a level 2. Each change is observed and discussed through an understanding and observation of the changes in speed and rhythm. Try this with different emotions.

Speed and rhythm of movement is the crux of the physical performance. From speed and rhythm we deduce status, intent, character, points of concentration etc.

Creating Inner monologues

The principal skill of mask actors is the communication of their inner monologue. It entails finding the speed and rhythm of movement that speaks their thoughts. Doing it unmasked may seem strange, but it pinpoints the moments when the actors think they are telling the audience something, but in fact are saying nothing. It also allows them to explore the idea of *clocking* the audience.

EXERCISE: CLEANING THE ELEPHANT

A simple exercise to start exploring inner monologue is the cleaning of the elephant. The actor is cleaning a large imaginary elephant. The exercise is interrupted by a noise made by the teacher, such as clapping hands. Here's the simple structure that goes from point to point without interruption. You will need to talk the students through each stage first however:

- The actor hears a noise, but ignores it. Only his head registers the noise.
- He hears it again, slows down the cleaning, but again doesn't stop cleaning. He looks in the direction of the noise and then goes back to normal speed.
- Again he hears the noise and he stops. Looks. He thinks. He cleans.
- Again the noise, he stops and moves towards the noise a short way. He pauses and then returns to his task.
- Finally the noise again. He stops, travels a way towards the noise. Pause, then a hurried return and a frantic restarting of his task.

This can be done both silently and with the hum of the vocalised inner monologue. Essentially this exercise is excellent for exploring and understanding the process of *Realisation, decision and reaction*. Work on the expanded moment realising the sound has happened, how the actor turns the head towards the sound etc. Then add the moments when the actor *clocks* the audience, to tell them what he or she is thinking. This might be when they hear the noise, or after they've moved each time towards the noise.

EXERCISE: CLOTHES

Put an array of objects and clothes around the stage, on tables and chairs. Let the actors find a simple character – probably themselves – and have them discover the items in the room. It could be their childhood room, or forgotten items in a loft. They could be sorting through things after a horrendous tragedy, to identify a loved one. They could be deciding what to send to a car-boot sale. There are two ways of playing this. First, silently. Imagine if it were a piece of film or television. The camera is in close, so the actors need to do very little to portray the inner workings of their mind. See how much the audience can understand without text. Now add the inner thoughts. Let an actor talk to himself throughout, and make sure he is saying things that he can communicate to an audience. If he says 'Blimey, look at that old scarf', he should be saying that to the audience, with a simple articulation of the body that goes with the verbal phrase. The thing to look out for is that they are not relying on the text, but are communicating physically. Later, when this exercise is repeated in masks, it should be much longer, since the thinking time of the mask is much slower than unmasked.

EXERCISE: OPERA

Start by asking the students to establish a simple domestic chore through action – painting the wall, doing the ironing etc. Get them to add a specific attitude to the movement, such as impatience, annoyance, glee etc. They now need to find the moments when they break off from the task and talk to us, the audience, with simple, clear thoughts. They need to find thoughts that can in some way be realised through action as well as text. The thoughts obviously need to be linked to their mood. The important point is for people to get the idea of physicalising an idea, rather than just telling us about it. The final development is to sing the thought in cod-grand opera – this focuses the actor onto the clarity of the thought, and the form of its expression.

The inner monologue could be seen as too complex an idea for younger students, and may want to be broached later on – the mask can still be taught without it. For the more experienced student it will immediately bring a psychological depth to the work. The benefits of this work become apparent when the masks are finally used. What we are aiming at are expanded moments of intense thought. There is a story about a famous Hollywood star who sends all scripts he receives out to readers. These scripts are then returned to him, with a number on the front. The higher the number, the more likely he is to read that script. The number? It's the number of times the main character makes an important decision. That is where the acting is, in the making of decisions. The star should have taken up mask theatre, for a mask actor is making decisions *all the time*!

Countermask

Countermask, as explained in Chapter 3, is playing an attitude or emotion counter to the one expressed on the mask and is a vital part of playing the mask successfully. There are some exercises one can do to prepare the actor, though in truth countermask is less about technicalities, and more about playing an emotional truth. Therefore, one learns about playing countermask actually in the mask. The 'Crossing the room' exercise is a good start to explaining to younger performers the simple way countermask works. Here's another one that also looks at physical timing.

EXERCISE: THE EYE!

On a table is a pile of clothes, and an upturned cup – preferably plastic. An actor enters with a strong attitude, both facial and physical; he's angry, forlorn, ecstatic etc. He's going home after a party and is searching for his keys, in the speed and rhythm of his emotional attitude. At some point he lifts the cup, under which (you have explained to him and the audience) is an eyeball. The actor reacts with a change in speed and rhythm, without (and this is the difficult bit) losing his initial facial expression. So Mr Angry reacts with a show of horror, or hysterics or fear, without losing the angry face. The actor makes an exit.

Focus

Controlling the focus of an audience is vital to making mask theatre work. Quite simply, the audience should know where to look at any one time. Split focus occurs when the audience are trying to look at something *when they shouldn't be!* Sometimes it is part of the action – a visual chord – that we ask the audience to take in several things at once. But generally, we want them to follow a flow of thought, of non-verbal communication and conversation around the stage.

The easiest way of describing the process is to say that the person whom we want the audience to look at is in *major*, while everybody else is in *minor*. Those in minor are supporting the person in major by

- looking at them – giving them the focus
- playing with a lower level of energy
- doing nothing to distract the audience.

It could be all or just one of the above. The focus passes from one person to another by several means.

- The major person passes it with eye contact – as if giving 'permission'.
- The person in minor takes it – increases energy or interest.

A surefire way for a mask to take the focus is for it to look at the audience directly, almost as if demanding their attention. The process and reasoning behind focus is very easy to grasp, and also to ignore. Therefore, a director must be vigilant in ensuring that the audience are seeing the right thing at the right time. It is very easy, with visual storytelling, for an audience to miss vital clues through the bad management of focus. Here are a couple of simple exercises to ensure that everybody understands the process.

EXERCISE: PRISONERS

Groups of students are arranged around the room, between four and seven in a group. They are prisoners escaping from their cells and their objective is to cross the room. Only one person in each group can move at any one time, making imaginary corridors, rooms and doors, but all the groups move at once. The person in each group moving is in major, while the others in the group are supporting them by giving them the focus, and are in minor. After a short distance, the person in major stops and passes the focus, through eye contact, to somebody else in the group, who can then move. The group has to get themselves all across the room pretty much together. At some point there will be chaos, as all the groups pass each other in the middle of the room. The teacher or observer should be able to watch the exercise and always know which person in each group has the focus.

EXERCISE: THE LINE-UP

A more advanced exercise: between four and six people are in a line facing the audience. The person on the left-hand side, directly to the audience, starts to express a simple emotion – a little laugh or a tremor of fear, a mutter of anger etc. This person is in *major*, while everybody is looking at them in *minor*. The focus is then passed to the next person in the line through eye contact, and is taken by engaging with the audience. The emotion increases slightly. The focus passes again down the line, each time it being very clear who has focus, when it is passed, and who is in *minor*. The emotion builds each time. When it gets to the end, without a break in tension, the focus is passed back to the person at the beginning of the line, by the last person leaning forward and engaging eye contact. The exercise continues round and round until it collapses or you feel that no more can be achieved. This exercise should get fairly hysterical, though there are several things to look out for. The energy should always rise. The important learning point here is that those in *minor* do not switch off until it is their turn to 'perform', but instead keep the emotion bubbling away at a lower level until their turn; it is easier for them to launch the laugh etc. when their energy is up, and it is more interesting to watch. Be aware of dropped or split focus.

The rising emotion will at some point exceed the vocal capabilities of the actors, so ensure they understand that the physical representation is as important. This is a very exposing exercise, but works well if people throw themselves into it. It may help to give the performers a particular focus, such as something terrifying behind the audience, or watching a very funny film. When running this exercise I find myself leaping around the stage conducting the actors!

Further character work

There are many different exercises to encourage the performer to think about character in terms of physical presence, speed and rhythm. Observation is an excellent tool, and can be easily applied in the classroom or studio. The following exercise is easy to set up, but if you feel more adventurous, the work we did in Trestle's early life was going on to the streets and observing the public. We returned to the rehearsal room to share our discoveries. It is interesting observing other ages and sexes, and trying to create a realistic interpretation rather than a cartoon. The other favourite, particularly for drama schools, is to spend time in the zoo. Each person is allocated an animal, which they have to observe and then recreate back in the rehearsal room. The next step is to find the physical essence of the animal and to turn that into a human character. It is not about making a man from a horse, but about physicalising characteristics. A horse can be portrayed by its impetuous and head-tossing nature, which when revealed through human behaviour creates a character that is essentially human, through which one could glimpse the source animal.

EXERCISE: PASTICHE

The pastiche exercise involves the random pairing up of performers. One is 'A', the other 'B'. A walks around the room as normally as possible, ignoring any instructions given to B. B follows A closely observing every aspect of A's movement, from its general rhythm and speed, to the specifics of how all the joints articulate, how the head is carried, the attitude in the back etc.

After a brief period of observation from different angles, and from following, B should start to mimic A's walk as best as possible. A drops out of the exercise and watches (in horror) at the cruel impersonation. It is now time to play! B should start to take the mickey, indulging the movement and picking on a particular feature of it. Keep pushing it to its limits. Then suddenly pull it back to as best a pastiche as they can manage – as normal as possible.

Now reverse the As and Bs. At the end of the exercise, make sure everybody apologises to each other.

Character sources are all around us, in the elements, animals, plants, even in the colours of the rainbow. (Think green. What is the character of green? What are its mood, its rhythm etc?) Lecoq is the master of these various impetuses for character, and his book *The Moving Body* (2000) explains many of the creative ways that he has gone about working with students, before or without the use of text.

Sound

Start developing the idea of finding a voice for a character, even if that voice is going to remain silent behind the mask. It is vital that actors have a voice in their head, to which they can play along with, finding the right gestural speed and rhythm to match the character's thinking.

EXERCISE: THE SOUND OF THE MASK

Hold a mask up to the group. Let them find a physical attitude that goes with the facial expression, and then let them experiment with sound. At first the noise will be barely human, consisting of grunts and exclamations. But words soon appear, and as actors relax into the voice they have found, along with a simple speed and rhythm of movement, they can start to interact. In discovering the voice of the character, one discovers the phrases, the asides, the speech pattern, and ultimately the internal rhythm of the character. This is so important, because in order to discover the physical truth, one needs to know the weight and length of the verbal phrases. The physical phrase matches the verbal one. For instance, if a character contemptuously dismisses someone, the actor needs to be very clear what the words are he is inferring, to make the gesture seem real, and for the audience to 'hear' those words for themselves.

None of the above is essential pre-mask work, but if the students or actors are inexperienced at working physically it allows them to communicate in a new way, paving the way for the shock of putting on the mask for the first time.

If nothing else, the following exercise is the simplest way of preparing to put the mask on.

EXERCISE: PULLING THE FACE

As above, hold the mask up to the group. Get them to pull the face of the mask on their own face. From this, encourage them to get a feeling for the character that emanates from and is based in the chest. The attitude of the chest reflects the emotion in the mask. From this, a physical attitude should become apparent, which can be revealed by simply asking the actors to walk around, finding the speed and rhythm of the mask. This is the closest you can get to working initially in a mask, without actually putting it on! Work fast, and use different masks in quick succession. The idea is to work instinctively and organically rather than intellectually.

CHAPTER 6

Using the Mask

The first moments

The objective of the first encounter with the mask is to bring a character to life as realistically and truthfully as possible. If one sets more goals than that, the simplicity of the moment will be clouded by the actor's desire to be funny, tell a story etc. All one wants to achieve at first is to put the mask on and simply exist in the space.

To aid the moment, remind the performer of the cardinal sin of mask work: *never* let the audience know that you are just an actor wearing a mask. Aim to have them completely believe in the transformation. Simple giveaways are:

- too much gesture, signalling a lack of speech
- sounds from behind the mask
- movements totally out of character, or not of the moment, such as adjusting the mask
- being too close to the front row.

This last one is interesting. As a demonstration, tell the audience you are going to put the mask on and walk towards them. Ask them to shout 'Stop!' when they feel the mask is close enough. Then stand at the back of the stage area, facing away from the audience, and put a mask on. Turn around, let the audience react and then walk slowly (in character) towards them until you hear someone ask you to stop. Invariably it is about 6–8 feet from the front row. Ask them why they shouted stop, and generally their responses will encapsulate how the mask works. These include:

- It didn't seem real any more.
- I could only see the face.
- I was suddenly aware of the mask.

That magic distance of 6–8 feet allows the audience to connect with and believe in the mask. Any closer and they become aware of the artifice, the contradictions between mask and skin. They feel let down. There is also the sense of being overwhelmed, trying to process visual information that rapidly changes as the mask gets closer, going from one sense of reality to another. Heady stuff!

Putting the mask on

This is it. Ask the first person to sit on the floor with their back to the audience. If it is possible, when working with a younger age group, try working with a blank wall in front of them. Give them the mask, and ask them to look at it, to pull the face of the mask on their own face. From that expression, an internal sense of the character comes, even if the facial impersonation is not great. Ask them to think about the speed and rhythm of the character and to have a sound in their head that is the 'voice' of the character. That is all they need to think about. Now get them to put the mask on, spending a few moments to adjust the mask to get comfortable and to get the hair, where possible to dress the front of the mask or to cover the elastic.

Ask them to stand up, but not turn around. Place yourself among or behind the audience if possible. Ask the mask to turn round and face the crowd. If you have a young performer, and a blank wall available, ask them to touch the wall and to keep touching it even when they have turned around. This denies them the opportunity to over-gesticulate. Invariably they will get a laugh from their mates

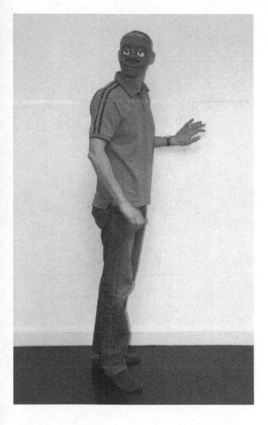

Figure 6.1 A mask's
first moment

as they turn round. In this, the first go at putting the mask on, the exercise follows a simple hot-seating process, though it can be easily embellished.

Hot-seating

The trick with hot-seating is to ask the right questions. Try to find questions to which they must give an emotional response, as well as offer opportunities for them to discover things about their character, to play *countermask*. Finding a range of emotional responses, moving into countermask, should be easily achievable in this first exercise.

EXAMPLE 1: A HAPPY MASK

'Hello. Are you all right?'
They nod enthusiastically.

'That's great. Find somewhere great to stand on the stage.'
They look about and choose a spot.

'Oooh, are you sure, is that the best place for you to stand?'
They look again, try somewhere else.

'Are you sure now?'
They are or aren't convinced.

'Are you pleased to be here?'
Oh yes!

'Really! I thought you hated the dentist?'
They respond accordingly.

'Because, as you know, it can get really painful, lots of blood and things.'
Give them space to react.

'I thought you were being very brave about it'.
I am. I'm very brave.

'You are brave? Show us then.'
Maybe they strike a pose.

'Well, you've certainly impressed somebody in the room. I happen to know somebody here really fancies you.'
They respond in a variety of ways!

'Maybe you could do something to impress them.'
They try.

'Oh dear, they appear to have left the room.'

EXAMPLE 2: A SAD MASK

'Hello. Come in please.'
They morosely come on and sit in the chair centre stage.

'Excuse me! Did I say sit?'
They respond.

'Well, don't do it again. You may sit.'
They respond.

'You're not looking too happy today.'
They respond.

'Have you been stood up again?'
They respond.

'You need to smarten yourself up a bit . . .'
They respond.

'Well, maybe cheer up then. Try and be happy. Think of something happy.'
They respond.

'Now imagine you've seen someone you really like. Attract their attention.'
They respond.

'I think it's working.'
They respond.

'Yes, they're walking over to you. Stand up, quick, ask them to dance.'
They respond.

'Yes, they . . . oh . . . they're with someone else . . .'
They respond.

'Sorry about that. Better luck next time . . .'

Figure 6.2 **On the hot-seat**

There are certain simple topics, such as birthdays, lack of card and presents etc., or pets – the death or loss of – which can push simple triggers to promote countermask. Give the novice a couple of minutes on stage. The important thing here is not to love your own voice too much, but to give the actor space to create and develop ideas. Provoke them if they get stuck. Tell them that everything they've said so far has been a lie. Ask the performer to leave the stage, asking them to play to us as long as possible. Next up is a brief appraisal of how they did.

Group analysis

As stated earlier, much of the learning takes place in the audience, so it is important to elicit their response to the work immediately. What worked? What didn't work? What are the reasons? What was the best bit? Any comments for the performer? It is also useful to ask for the performer's response to wearing the mask for the first time.

What we are trying to get the audience to realise is when they felt the most connection with the mask. This is the moment when the mask thinks, when the movement seems to be in inverted commas. It is the moment of *realisation, decision and reaction*. What should be apparent after several goes is that the change in movement that expresses the most is the change in *speed and rhythm*.

Group work

Hot-seating can be done in ones or twos, playing characters off against each other. Bigger groups require a different exercise, but this is useful if you have less time, or your performers are more experienced and you want to go into deeper work quicker.

EXERCISE: ENTRANCES AND EXITS

Start with simple entrances and exits, getting characters to enjoy the game of revealing themselves to an audience and then taking their leave. Put music over the top of it. They should try to find different speeds and rhythms that will give them different attitudes, without having to try and create a logical narrative. It is just about coming on and going off.

Eventually assemble them all on the stage.

Ask them to find the best place to stand etc.

Then do 'The lesson' exercise.

EXERCISE: THE LESSON

This involves asking the group simple questions that they need to try and answer, such as

- Who is the most beautiful?
- Who is the ugliest?
- Who is the bravest?
- Who is the strongest?
- Who is the cleverest?

Encourage the masks not only to think about themselves, but also to point out other people. Develop interactions by asking characters to show their bravery or their intelligence, or to tell you which is the most beautiful part of them etc.

This simple exercise allows you to provoke the masks into making decisions through realisations. Talk to the masks individually to give them the focus and so that the others know what is going on.

Figure 6.3 The Lesson

If you are working in a large group, it is often a good idea to pair people up. This allows you not only to share masks, but also to work with one group working on stage, and the other group to observe their partner and make notes. Regroup after each go to exchange feedback. You can also use this method to do initial hot-seating, with the pairs all working at once in a larger space. Here are some more group impros. Most of these can lead on from an entrances and exits game.

EXERCISE: THE USUAL SUSPECTS

Tell the group that they've all been found guilty of a terrible crime, and are to be put to death. Only one person was responsible, but we can't find out which one, so we're just going to execute everybody. Would anybody like to confess, grass a mate etc. Any martyrs? Finally announce that they've all been fed a poison that is now starting to work. Allow the characters to die very slowly, trying to keep both character and dignity intact to the end. Music works very well with this.

EXERCISE: THE DANCING COMPETITION

Thank them all for coming to the auditions for a televised dancing competition. Get them to dance to music in a variety of ways:

- showing off to a loved one
- dancing when you know you shouldn't be
- dancing in a very crowded disco
- dancing your last dance
- dancing when somebody has just laughed at your dancing.

EXERCISE: BOMB DISPOSAL

An old Trestle favourite! Wrap an ad hoc choice of objects in newspaper and place them on the floor. Tell the masks that they are at the bomb disposal final exam. They are to treat the packages as suspect, and to finally unwrap them without any going off. Provoke them constantly, question their methods, hear tick-tocking etc. Once opened, the game turns into . . . 'Presents'.

EXERCISE: PRESENTS

These objects are special presents for them from a loved one. Let them unwrap them. What do they think of them? Are they pleased? Does anybody want to swop? What can they use their present for, other than its intended use? Finally (and perversely) ask them to tell us what they think of their mother by the way they use their object.

Many things become apparent in these exercises that it is hoped will be acknowledged. First, improvising in a mask in a group is very difficult and very messy. Focus is invariably split, people communicate with others without permission, people bump into each other, miss things etc. But good things do happen, it is invariably entertaining, and everybody has the experience of wearing the mask and expressing themselves through it. Second, people will invariably come in and out of character all the time. Wearing a mask is uncomfortable, and the actor must overcome the factors of sweat, breathing and poor vision to maintain the mask's integrity.

In a bid to increase skills and awareness of the mechanics of mask acting, now is a good time to repeat the 'Cleaning the elephant' exercise (p. 59) in the masks, with people out front watching their partners and then commenting on their effectiveness. It becomes apparent very quickly whether or not somebody has a clear, logical and economic thought process, and whether or not the verbal and physical phrases are compatible.

Big groups

We don't all have the luxury of time or a small, focused group of students. For instance, suppose you want to introduce a class of thirty 14 year olds to the possibilities of masks but you have only a one-hour session to do it in. How then to get everybody in a mask in that time? The pre-mask exercises can be done in large numbers anyway, but here are some initial mask exercises for the larger group.

EXERCISE: LEAVING HOSPITAL

Split the group in half and make one lot the audience, the others arranged offstage and in masks. Each character makes an entrance, traverses the stage from upstage *left* to downstage *right* and exits. Give the group simple emotional stories to communicate. For instance, each person is a new Dad leaving hospital after the birth of . . . well . . . say, quins! They can communicate the mixture of elation, horror, surprise, confusion etc. during their brief journey. Get them to work on the stops, pauses, the thinking moments that lead us through the character's realisations and reactions. They may enter exhausted, stop, realise they are a father, and feel very proud, then it dawns on them they now have five children to feed, feel rather daunted and nervous, and exit counting the money in their wallet.

This simple format can be repeated with a different scenario. The person leaves hospital having been told they have only weeks to live. Halfway across the stage their phone rings. They answer it and are told to check the lottery slip in their pocket. They've won a million! How do they exit? Get a simple bandage and have the person walk on blindfold, then they stop and remove the bandage. It's worked! They can see! They take a mirror from their pocket and see themselves for the first time. How do they react? They then exit and hand the props on to the next person waiting on the other side – or maybe they turn around and want to be made blind again!

EXERCISE: FOOTBALL FANS

Rival football fans pass in the street after the match. How are their opposite fortunes expressed. You could do this in pairs, each person with a red or blue scarf which is then handed on to the next person in the wings. How do the different characters cope with success or failure? What does a morose person on the winning team do to the happy person who has lost? Encourage the students to surprise us with their reactions.

This can be tried in larger groups, though it might be worth having some organisation first, an agreement between each team about their reactions.

EXERCISE: GETTING LOST

A very simple exercise that can get through the numbers easily but that still offers the participants plenty of scope for individuality. The mask enters with purpose but halfway across the stage doubt sets in. Is it going the right way? Does it recognise where it is? Play a scene of 'Getting lost', and encourage the actors to consider not just the practicalities of being lost, but also the emotional ones – the embarrassment, fear, anger, panic etc.

Short improvisations

The work develops through applying these skills to short engineered impros. It is a good idea to work in small groups and to assign one person in each group to be the outside eye, the facilitator or director. If needs be, start by hot-seating the masks. Then try putting the masks into simple situations with clear objectives.

- A dance. A wants to get off with B, but B is waiting for someone else.

- A park bench. A is asleep on the bench. B wants to get A off and sleep, but A refuses to shift.
- A wants B to go and buy A a pint of milk. B refuses. How far can this impro go without making the audience aware of the lack of speech?

You can make hundreds of these little scenarios simply by manufacturing people's wants. They are short, and test the non-verbal communication skills of the actor, examining their resourcefulness in the face of Lecoq's *via negativa*.

EXERCISE: PING-PONG

The idea of this is to encourage the idea that masks can 'converse', without resorting to gesture and making the audience aware they can't speak. It also works the idea of focus, of being generous enough to allow the audience to watch the other person for a bit. It's called 'Ping-pong' because the audience's focus passes from one mask to the other like ping-pong. Make sure that the conversation is complete i.e. that the person not 'speaking' is giving their focus to the other mask, to allow the audience and them to 'hear' what has been said

- Have two masks on stage, with opposing objectives. Person A wants Person B to read a letter from A that says 'I'm leaving you'. Person B doesn't want to read the letter, but wants A to sit beside B and watch television.
- Person A wants person B to have a drink with A. Person B wants person A to play cards.
- Simply play a concentrated game, such as cards or pick-up-sticks, that involves each person 'having a go'.

EXERCISES: OBJECTS

Masks love to play with things, and the audience can read a great deal about the psychology of a character through its manipulation of the objects around the space. If it is most intriguing watching a character trying *not* to show an emotion, then it is through the manipulation of objects that the masks betrays itself.

- A mask enters a room with an assortment of objects around. They have a suitcase, and they start to pack the objects away. The speed and rhythm of movement allow us to create reasons for the scene. Another character enters and sits at the side and watches the packing, without seeming to comment. What is their attitude? How do looks between the characters affect the packing? Having packed, the first mask leaves. How does the second react knowing they are on their own? How do they leave?
- A pile of clothes, shoes and objects are strewn about the stage. A group of masks enter at speed and see the detritus – this is all that is left of their village after some terrible event. How do they react to each other, to the objects and clothes etc? How truthful can they be? Maybe give them an objective which is to finally exit with one piece of clothing or object. How do they choose? What is the significance of it? What happens when somebody else wants it too? This exercise, as in the previous one, can have music added to it. Try the exercise with just one person.

EXERCISE: CLOTHING

Allow a group of masks to rifle through an assortment of costumes and hats, choosing something for their character. End up with a costume parade. These costumes can then be used in future exercises, adding colour and depth to the characters. Hats work particularly well, especially soft hats.

Figure 6.4 The Packing exercise

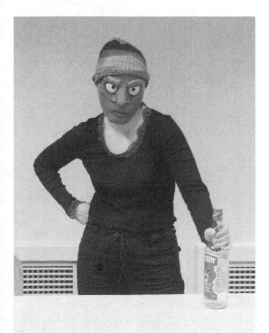

Figure 6.5 Hats and props

Expanded moments

All these initial exercises cover the basic skills of communicating character, thought, emotion etc. truthfully, and playing the counter-mask successfully. When the students are showing a good grasp of these skills they can start to explore what I called the 'expanded moments', which somehow seem to be a hallmark of the mask. These moments exist around the thoughts, realisations, decisions and reactions of the characters, but that become imbued with a greater significance and emotional weight. They somehow become more filmic, as though the camera has gone in close and slowed everything down. It's not that more is being said, but it's about the timing of the saying of it that lends it greater weight. I use the analogy of the old chest expander, the springs that you could pull apart to work your muscles. At rest, the spring is floppy and without tension, but it is still a spring. But if you pull it apart, expand it, then it immediately gains greater tension – and it becomes longer. Nothing has been added to it but space and tension. In the mask this seems to work well as an idea. A moment is expanded, slowed down – not that you are acting slo-mo – but the timings of the mask's thoughts are somehow slower, more considered and therefore of greater significance. Don't let it get indulgent. The lesson here is to discover dramatically what is of importance to the character, and to enjoy it realising that.

EXERCISE: WAKING UP

Two very different masks are put onstage under a blanket, feet facing the audience. One character previously designated wakes up first. It is the morning after a night that they can't quite remember. Maybe they were drunk, or are now hungover etc. After a while they realise they are not alone. They peek under the blanket and tell us about how they feel about who is under the blanket. Eventually the second mask emerges. How does this person react to the situation? How do the two characters react to each other, to the inevitable realisation about the previous night's events? How can the scene resolve, or at least make an exit?

EXERCISE: THE BUS STOP

A mask enters and starts to wait. Their attitude is relaxed but in character. Then a second mask enters and stands apart, just watching the first person. This unsettles the first mask, who increasingly feels uncomfortable. Do they make some revelatory realisation? Eventually the first mask is forced to leave, and the second character takes their place at the bus stop. After a short while a third mask enters, stands apart and just watches, making the second character increasingly uncomfortable until they too leave . . . This can go on for as long as you want.

Music

I personally use much music to underpin many of the exercises where a vocal stimulation isn't needed. Music softens the harshness of silence, and adds to the emotional journey of the scene. I tend to favour music that is non-committal in its emotional sense, music that is usually 'minimal' in its style. Composers such as Michael Nyman, Arvo Pärt, Philip Glass, Yann Tiersen (*Amelie*), Graham Fitkin or the Penguin Café Orchestra provide a good soundtrack. Alternatively, classical music such as Bach's cello suites provide a backing that can absorb a variety of emotional impulses.

You can of course use very strong music – I like using film music, or opera, for the masks to play along with, or fight against.

This work can be continued and developed as much as is deemed appropriate. But ultimately, it has to develop into the creation of work, of short choreographed sketches arising from improvisation. Providing a student has the basic skills of an actor, a degree of confidence and control over their limbs, they should be able to reach a good level of proficiency quite quickly. It is the application of the skills that takes, quite simply, talent.

CHAPTER 7

Devising with Masks

Why devise? I have always devised with masks because that is the richest way of working with them. Sometimes certain pieces of theatre are called 'director's theatre' or 'writer's theatre'. Masks, if anything, are 'actor's theatre', though in truth at best they are always 'ensemble theatre'. Masks need to create their moments on the stage and can't be written for in great detail – that is, after all, what killed Commedia. But devising also allows you to tap into a broader range of creativities, all the people involved get to contribute. It is a process that can so easily spiral out of control, so I think it is worth asking the questions, 'Are you devising a project for the experience of the process, or for the outcome?' 'Is the project outcome focused or process focused?' There will be a difference in the way one structures the work and pursues ideas if you work out the answer to that question. Most school-based work is experiential, whereas with professional work one is trying to get the best show at the end of it, and the process must reflect that.

There are whole books on the devising process, and I don't intend to rewrite them here (see Oddey 1994; Lamden 2000). There are a few simple truths.

- The devising process is entirely dependent on the chemistry between the people in the room at the time. Different people coming and going will change the chemistry. This might be a good thing or it might be bad. But it is necessary to understand that the people involved will have the greatest influence on the process – it is not something that is all about the quality of the ideas and nothing else. It is about how people spark each other off, enthuse or infuriate. Some people just wind each other up – maybe the best of friends. Sometimes you discover someone has a completely different attitude to the work or the process than that which you were expecting. The principal skill of a leader or director is to be able to put the team together successfully, to make them creative, and (let's hope) happy!

- Once an idea has been spoken, it is no longer the property of the person who thought it, for they have planted seeds in other people's heads, and they can't take them back. Make sure this is understood, so that ideas can be released when ready, or are happily tossed into the fray. People can get very precious about their personal vision for something: 'That's not what I meant!' I remember working on a piece with a large group – 25 participants all told – on a two-week devising project. After two days one of the actors came in and made a statement about what he thought the show should be about, and then proceeded to read out a finished scenario he had been working on. We rejected it. He left immediately.

- Beware people – usually couples – who go home at night, discuss the project, and come in the next morning with a fait accompli, a journey fully travelled with either little opportunity for discussion, or little space for new ideas. Again, people get precious about ideas that seemed like the greatest thing the night before. Advise caution on discussion on the project unless everybody is present!

- Don't spend hours talking, get up and do! That is the only way to discover whether or not something works.

- Acknowledge by name where ideas come from: 'Let's try Robert's idea about the dead flowers'. People can get very precious when devising, as there is little space for individual recognition of creativity. Everything is a collaboration, and a consensus always needs to be reached. One is constantly compromising one's ideas.

Devised work has rarely had the cachet of its mainstream counterpart, the written script interpreted by the director. Something about too many cooks spoiling the broth. But creators such as Robert Lepage and Théâtre de Complicité have created some of the best theatre in the modern age through devising. The vital ingredient is the presence of a director – a facilitator if you like – who guides the creative team, acting as arbiter, dramaturg, provoker etc., but most of all, the outside eye which, in mask theatre, is a vital role. When working with masks, you need somebody to perform to. You should never rehearse to an empty room, for actors wearing masks know very little about the impact of their performance without somebody sitting there to experience it and to offer feedback. This is not necessarily to hand a position of power to the director, but to acknowledge that in the process of devising, where all creators consider themselves to have an equal voice, the director's job is to facilitate the process and to act as a brake to the excesses of the performer.

Directors should at some point consider who they are creating the work for – who are the audience?

A brief polemic: *Part Two* (on audiences)

Ah yes, the audience! Who are they? Well, they live in the here and now, so they are a modern audience. They are, no matter what age, influenced by the other media around them – television, advertising and cinema. They are visually literate. So why treat them as though they have ration books in their back pockets? Many of today's playwrights are still writing old plays, 'room' theatre that is created by the lone writer with little space for rehearsal ensemble input. The structure and presentation method of many new plays seems to be stuck in a mid-twentieth-century time warp. Everybody wants to be the new John Osborne or Harold Pinter. But in their day these writers were cutting edge, creating work that mirrored the new cinema world of Lindsay Anderson or Ken Loach. Today's playwrights need to consider the audience they are creating for, and have an awareness of the increased visual manner of much popular culture. It means presenting the work in a *form* that is relevant to their other experiences of entertainment, but that does not lose sight of the essential game of theatre.

In 2002 the National Theatre did a survey of the tastes of young people in south London. What did they want to see in the theatre? They were expecting the reply to be about modern-day subjects – drugs, unemployment, gangs, sex etc. What they got shocked them. The reply was 'Great soundtracks, and great images'. Nothing to do with *content* and everything to do with *form*. So I'm not advocating abandoning the back catalogue, or trying to present only gritty modern work. What I'd like to see is work created that acknowledges the visual development in our culture, the influence on our narratives of film and television. And the mask is well placed to be part of that work. If we consider the script to be an integral part – sometimes the first part – of the process, and not the last, then we can find a way of rediscovering plays for a modern audience.

Jumping form

One way of doing this is to embrace the idea that theatre can 'jump form' just as film and television do. While these media have a host of technological forms they can use, and with which we are conversant with – jump cuts, cross-fades, slo-mo, soundtracks, isolations, moving cameras and so on – theatre needs to find its own forms, and the ways of jumping between them. Even if text is the bedrock of a production, there are plenty of ways of telling the story visually, of having other forms at our fingertips. None of this is new, the forms aren't new, but many theatre-makers seemed to have forgotten that there are a number of tools in the toolbox, which have always been there. But the obsession with text, and the writer's inability to see beyond the spoken word, has led to a dull hegemony of the script that stifles creative theatre. My friend and mask-maker Russell Dean coined the phrase *trailing edge technology* to describe the way that we make theatre. I rather like that, and it sums up *Jumping form* as well. Let cinema be all high-tech. We create magic with bodies and bits of wood, cloth and rope. And with the great imaginations of our audience. What, then, am I talking about, exactly? Here is a rundown and explanation of forms that we can currently jump between.

Expanded moments

As mentioned earlier, the analogous chest expander can work as an idea on theatre in general. Halt the text and go somewhere else for a while, to heighten the emotional moment, reinforce the theme, tell another part of the narrative. In Trestle's production of *The Barretts of Wimpole Street* (2000), at the moment when Robert Browning first meets Elizabeth Barrett, I stopped the text and had Barrett turn to the audience like a dizzy schoolgirl and breathlessly recite her sonnet 'When I First Met Him'. When she finished she turned back to him and the play continued as if nothing had occurred. The moment was further heightened by a snap lighting change, and the appearance of a number of books pushed through the walls and animated to resemble birds in flight.

Change the scale

Change the scale of the action – usually through some sort of animation. In *Blood and Roses* (2001), I staged the Battle of Stoke Field (1487) in the kitchens of Henry VIII (where Lambert Simnel had been sent to work following the failure of his conspiracy). At the height of the battle the actors grabbed food and played out the scene on a table top, as though seen from high above. Spring onions became the flights of arrows, fish kebabs became the advancing troops. The soundtrack aided the moment by switching to the sound of wind – I asked the sound designer to create the sound of a kestrel hovering above the battle field!

Action

Action can be created away from the text, as can other characters. Again, in *The Barretts*, we added the characters of Elizabeth Barrett's dead mother and brother, pivotal characters in her life. We saw them as ghosts, picking up on her obsession with spiritualism, and who came to her at moments when Barrett was in a high emotional state, or trying to make a difficult decision. They aren't mentioned in the play.

Choreography or dance

Can something be added by turning to a more stylised form of presentation? Companies such as Frantic Assembly or DV8 or Volcano have used this to great effect. It is possible in masks too. I have found it a very useful way of showing another aspect of a relationship, or encapsulating a mood at a particular time. *The Barretts* had the father's text removed, and the character put into a full mask. Through our research we discovered that the scene towards the end when Elizabeth confronts her father, leading to a great row with sexual undertones, was historically inaccurate. As he couldn't speak I had Elizabeth respond to him as though he were talking to her, but they started following a route of choreography that saw her trying get him to read a letter, and to leave the room. The two ghosts appeared and manipulated the warring pair together, trying to reach some resolution. Father slammed doors, threw down letters, and over the top the soaring music of Thomas Tallis overpowered the text until a sudden moment of silence and stillness.

Music and soundtrack

Music is obviously very important, as important potentially as in film. Soundtrack too. It's not just something we hear between scenes. Sometimes music can say things better than text, or at least say them differently. Look at the way film uses the sound, the way scenes start aurally before they do visually, the way volume is used, or dichotomies are created through the choice of music clashing with an emotional moment. In *Tonight We Fly* (2003), the story of Marc Chagall, Chagall tries to say goodbye to his fiancée Bella (masked) at the station. There is live music happening at the time. I decided to have Chagall be unable to open the carriage window as the train pulled out, so we saw him declaring his love for her and his determination to return, purely through expansive gesture, done in perfect time to a wild euphonium solo played in the window next to him.

Visual chords

We can create visual chords, several things happening at once, some with text, some without. It is a good way of consolidating moments in a story, or creating tension before a climax. It also creates a number of different moods. It is like a split screen on television.

Animation

Animation exists in many forms, from puppetry or shadow work, to object manipulation. They offer changes in scale and perspective, allowing you to see new characters, idiosyncratic moments, or to stage things that the human body can't do. In *Beyond the Blue Horizon* (1997), I wanted to see a vast desert, with a man crawling across it, with a camel train appearing. The entire stage became the desert floor, and a twelve-inch puppet showed us the man crawling along, operated from beneath the stage in a long thin trap. The camel appears. As they exit the real size man appears crawling on from the other side, followed by a full-sized camel!

Mime and physical theatre

Mime and physical theatre enable us to do many things, including creating environments quickly and effectively, through illusion and sound. We can be hanging from a cliff face, standing in a church, walking through a meadow, or a forest, simply by manipulating bodies in space. We need to understand the audience's desire to believe magic, and to acknowledge the power of the human body. One of my top five shows of all time was Trevor Nunn's *Nicholas Nickleby* (1982). I was pleased to see that some scenes were created almost entirely through mime, such as a crowd pressing their noses up to the glass of a pie shop, before switching to being the rich people inside the shop eating the merchandise.

Multi media

Multi media is less 'trailing edge technology', and more a minefield unless you are well set up for it. I went to see a major show at the Edinburgh Festival that was cancelled because a bolt had broken, and a show in London that was postponed because a video lead was faulty. But technology leaps forward all the time and the use of film and video becomes increasingly easier to use. The difficulty comes in integrating it successfully. It can also be a very expensive medium, and needs to be done very well, as we have an expectation of the projected or recorded arts that is partly due to the expense of them. But they can still be *trailing edge*. In the Frantic Assembly/Paines Plough show *Tiny Dynamite* (2001), two men argue over a map as they drive along, with their journey projected onto the back of the map. Simple, but very sweet.

Er . . . masks?

There may be other forms. There are definitely different ways of jumping between them, and one need only jump between two forms to make something more interesting. But first we need to get our heads round a very important fact:

The text is not sacrosanct!

The process of creation does not end with the delivery of the text. We have a culture of reverence towards the writer, who delivers the play after many drafts in consultation maybe with a dramaturg. But the expectation thereafter is that the text will then be staged as it is writ! This need not be the case, everything is movable. The Bosnian director Mladen Materic put it brilliantly. He said that text is just the black box voice recording of an event.

The black box

An aeroplane crashes in Russia, and the black box is recovered. They reconstruct the final moments of the plane, as they hear the recording of Gregor, the co-pilot, arguing with the pilot, Ivan. Gregor is shouting at Ivan to sit down, stop playing with this or that button, to do as he is told. Ivan has clearly gone mad, and crashed the plane. That is what the 'text' says. However, Ivan's body is not in the cockpit, but in the back of the plane. In the cockpit is the body of a young boy. This too is Ivan, Gregor's 6-year-old son. Gregor has allowed him to fly the plane and it has gone wrong. The plane has crashed.

So the text says one thing, but the action of the event is open to interpretation. Many British writers are fearful of this creative intervention, but I believe the collaboration between writer, director, designer and actor is the only way to produce the best modern theatre. Collaboration in cinema and television is an accepted way of working, many people working together on projects, adding ideas to the pot. For me, the collaboration of Sergio Leone and Ennio Morricone in producing spaghetti westerns is a prime example. Morricone did not produce the music to a finished film, but wrote the music for the script, which was recorded and put onto record. Leone then worked with actors and camera operators in the desert, with the record beside him playing away. The action was choreographed to the music.

So we need to encourage directors to give full vent to their imaginations, not only to think about their audience, but also to think about challenging them. We need to encourage writers to write new plays, not the old plays they turn out at the moment, which means looking at form, not content, and looking at the process of collaboration. If we want writers to write for masks they have to realise that what they write is just part of the process. Masks are a truly collaborative tool – performer, director, writer . . . audience. Masks are the oldest form of human performance and they have a place in the twenty-first century. They are one of the forms that theatre has to express its ideas and stories. They are visual, cheap, immediate, a folk art too long hidden away in museums and textbooks. In trying to make modern theatre, theatre for a modern audience, I think it perfectly natural that one should consider the mask and its associated form, the puppet.

Atmosphere

No matter what type of work you are creating, if you are using masks you have at your disposal the facility to really work on the atmosphere of a scene – sometimes all you need is a good atmosphere, something so intriguing that the audience are compelled to watch when in fact very little is happening. What makes atmosphere? It can be a combination of things, but tension is paramount, with unsaid thoughts, unexpressed emotions, an untold story, a suspension of a moment, all are in there in the mix. Here is an excellent exercise that allows you to both explore atmosphere, and acknowledge what exactly it is. This was created by Joff Chafer.

EXERCISE: THE FIVE POINTS

This exercise can be done in or out of masks, with or without music. And it really needs an audience to observe. Identify and number five points on the stage, using the occasional chair or table, or use the scenery of the play you are working on. One of the points could be offstage. Have a handful of actors to do the exercise. Ask them to have in their heads an order of five numbers, from 1 to 5. So they might have 51423, or 15234 etc. Get them to stand at the place on stage that corresponds to the first number in their sequence. So if their order is 35241, their first position will be number 3. The exercise now starts. The whole group must move all together, *in neutral*, to their next position. They pause for a breath, then move to their next position. Pause then move, pause then move. After they have gone through their five numbers, they start again at the beginning of the order, and keep going cyclically. It should have an odd quality to it, as though the stage were breathing in and out.

You can stop it after a few rounds and ask the audience's response to it. Did they make up stories? You can now continue, but throw in *points of concentration*. This means asking them to concentrate completely on one thing. For instance, ask everyone on stage to stare at one of the actors, never taking their eyes off them. Ask that actor to portray a simple attitude to the situation, remembering that trying *not* to show the attitude is more interesting. It might be guilt, glee, sorrow etc. Without stopping you can command them to throw the focus onto someone else, with a new attitude. So 'Everyone watch Jane. You feel sorry for her. Jane, you are angry with everyone.' Or 'Everyone watch Peter. You are furious with him. Peter, you are dismissive towards them.' How can music affect these scenes? What creates a good atmosphere? An extension would be to give the cast a definite story, out of the audience's earshot. So you could say, 'You're all friends, staying together. Jane has made an accusation of rape against Peter.' Let the exercise continue with that stimulus, or others that involve two people at odds with each other, but the audience need to fathom the story. Much of the learning in this exercise takes place in the audience, as they realise how much can be said to an audience by doing very little. It is all about suggestion.

Figure 7.1 The Five Point exercise, Roz Paul, Simon Grover, Joff Chafer and Alan Riley

Speed, rhythm and tension all help create atmosphere. See the 'Tension states' in Chapter 5.

Objectives

Another way of creating material that is non-verbal, as well as building atmosphere, is to have characters pursuing very clear objectives, but through strategies that make the objectives seem quite opaque. The important thing to remember here is that we can go well beyond naturalism, whereas people's natural inclination is to stick with the known and everyday.

'One goes to the theatre to find life, but if there is no difference between life outside the theatre and life inside, then theatre makes no sense. There's no point in doing it. But if we accept that life in the theatre is more visible, more vivid than on the outside, then we can see that it is simultaneously the same thing and somewhat different.'

Peter Brook, *There are No Secrets* (1993)

The master of this work is Mladen Materic, and I shall lay out some of his exercises here for you now. Materic has the luxury of extremely long rehearsal periods. He told me he will rehearse only a few hours a day, but for up to six months. This way the actors can get through the safe material and start to really fly with the improvisations. Good theatre, says Materic, should be like a well-wired plug. You need the earth wire, the thing that is grounded, rooted in human experience, our everyday lives. But you also need the live wire, the sparky, wild, dangerous, unexpected, theatrical element to lift the work off the stage and out of the humdrum.

Physicalising objectives helps us understand what we mean by objectives, and allows us to realise that drama isn't always made up of pure clashing objectives, but that there are levels of conflict. Materic describes it as physicalising Stanislavski. Much of Trestle's work, created in the rehearsal room by improvisation, has been done by simply following the idea of giving characters their objectives, and exploring the level of conflict between them, and the strategies they employ to achieve their goal. Here's a simple game to explore strategy.

EXERCISE: STRATEGY

With a group, usually of about ten or more people, ask them to take a chair and sit on it in an open space, facing any which way they like. Ask one person to leave their chair and stand at the opposite side of the room. They must now *walk* to their chair, to sit in it, but they can be foiled by somebody else getting up and sitting in their chair. But doing this frees up another chair, which the person can now try and fill, but can be stopped by somebody else getting up and sitting in that chair . . . get the idea? The person must walk, but everybody else can run. The game is usually over very quickly because people whizz out of their chairs to stop the person sitting down in the chair they are heading towards, not realising they've left a vacant chair right beside them. So a strategy needs to be employed, where the empty chair is filled by someone not close to it. It's a game of dizzy kippers really, but good fun. You could enforce the rule that once you've jumped up out of your chair, you can't return to it immediately.

Now we can explore the idea of characters working through strategy. This next exercise is also excellent at highlighting the essential ingredient of theatre – intrigue! Once the exercise starts you will probably notice that the actors go straight to their objectives and the whole thing quickly descends into a mess. If this happens, stop them and talk about how much more tantalising they could be if they were more subtle. If necessary tell them that at first they must not move from their seats and can use only their eyes! Here's the exercise.

EXERCISE: A WANTS B NOT C

Five to eight chairs are set in a line facing the audience. One person sits in each. Each person decides for themselves one person they are desperate to get close to, and one person they are keen to stay away from. Don't let them tell you who is who. Start the exercise by asking the actors to pursue their two objectives. This is where they charge about in a melee, so stop it and start again (see section on 'Relevation' later on). Encourage understatement and subtlety. Use eyes at first, or diversionary tactics. How *intriguing* can they be?

EXERCISE: FIVE POINTS DEVELOPMENT

Using the five point exercise again, add in elements of the objectives exercise, 'A wants B not C'. So the participants have clear objectives, and different subtle strategies for pursuing their objectives, but are tied into a random movement sequence that alternately confounds and fulfils their wants. Try coming up with different imagined locations, such as a school classroom during break time, or the front room during a family event, such as a funeral. Or a wedding!

Figures 7.2 and 7.3 A wants B not C exercise

Here's a Materic exercise for understanding both the physicalising of objectives, and the different levels of conflict that exist.

EXERCISE: MOULDING

In pairs, ask A to mould or sculpt B, with no particular intention other than moving B's limbs about. B is compliant, and does as he or she is asked. This is very boring, there is no drama, no conflict. A has an objective – to sculpt B, but meets no resistance. So we now introduce levels of conflict that isn't true conflict, because one person is enacting upon the other's objective, rather than pursuing his or her own objective.

So ask B to *ignore* A's objective. If A is trying to sculpt B, what does B do that frustrates A's objective by ignoring it? Maybe they walk away, sit down, get undressed etc. All they are doing is ignoring A, rather than definitely trying to do something different themselves. Now ask B to *misinterpret* A's objective. So if A lifts B's arm up, B might think A wants them to wave to someone. A moves a leg, B starts to dance. A's objective is being frustrated through misinterpretation.

Ask B to *avoid* A's objective, which is not the same as 'ignore'. A tries to lift B's arm, but B moves the arm so A can't hold it etc. Again A's objective is frustrated.

Finally, ask B to *resist* A's objective. So A tries to lift the arm but B stays rigid, resisting at all costs.

To create true conflict one can now give B an objective – to mould A. Let A start the moulding, then let B start trying to mould A. They start fighting, which is as simple a picture of conflict one can imagine – people with opposing objectives.

This can now be carried into text. A asks B to go and buy them a pint of milk. Go through the process of B *ignoring, avoiding, misinterpreting and resisting* the objective. Encourage people to be as creative as possible. Go beyond 'soap opera' acting!

Revelation

If you have clear objectives and strategies, then at some point you want the audience to be aware of them. As stated earlier, the inexperienced student will be rather gauche in the revelation of important dramatic material, going for the sudden hit. This I term the '*flasher*', where the revelation satiates the actor, who thinks they are doing something great, but that leaves the audience rather uninspired and uninvolved! Far better to be a '*stripper*', where the revelation is clearly for the audience's benefit, and there is at least some sense of dramatic tension, a calculated understanding of what audiences want. In a mask, where the audience are providing the dialogue, taking them on a journey that is unexpected and full of surprises and that is delicious in nature is far more satisfying for the audience than being told everything straight off, with no mystery at all.

The task now is to create improvisations that explore these ideas, both in and out of masks. First off, here's a good text exercise.

EXERCISE: THE RESTAURANT

A couple meet in a restaurant, but you have set up clear objectives beforehand, not telling A's objective to B, and vice versa. They are a couple who have been together for two years. A wants them to go onto the next stage and get married, have kids, buy a house etc. B thinks they are going nowhere and should split up. How interesting, how *delicious* can they make it for the audience?

It is easy to make up more of these scenes, working in a way, through text that the participant will find familiar. So now move it into a text-free zone! First off is an exercise that explores the levels of conflict without resorting to two sets of objectives.

Figures 7.4a–7.4d Moulding

EXERCISE: THE LETTER

A and B are a couple sharing a house, in a relationship. B wants to split up, but can't say it, so has written it down in a letter. B wants A to read the letter. A knows what is coming, so doesn't want to read the letter, ignoring, resisting, avoiding, misinterpreting B's desire for A to read the letter.

This exercise can be done in masks, but you need to go through the process of it being really messy in masks, and therefore rehearsing in and out of them. Again it is simple to think up a scene that contains an objective that is going to cause a level of conflict. With masks, what one is looking for are scenes that don't have speech at their heart, scenes that can be realised silently but with intense action.

EXERCISE: SCENES OF CONFLICT

A comes in to pack a suitcase. B observes at first and then tries to stop or waylay A. This scene can be applied to a number of situations:

- It is a child's room. What has happened?
- A is leaving B.
- A is packing B's things so B can leave.

In the mask, the objects will always take on a particular piquancy and tension. What do the objects mean to A and B? Where is the atmosphere in the scene? What effect does music have?

You might have noticed that these exercises produce quite serious drama! Masks can be comic and tragic, but it is much easier creating comic work for specific characters and situations, such as in an *observation* piece. The idea of exploring objectives is useful both in terms of honing the skills of the mask actor, as well as thinking about what a mask piece is actually going to be made of, what are its constituent parts. How, then, to go about creating work for the stage? The initial decisions that need to be made are concerned with style, content, convention, and format. A good place to start is with a short comic observation sketch.

Observation

Creating an observation piece is the easiest way of making mask theatre. You need to find a situation, familiar to some degree, where a range of characters may meet or pass through. You might already have decided to look at a particular group of people that makes this decision for you – such as an old people's home, or a crèche, or a staff room! Essentially you are looking for a location where action can develop, where crises can occur, where people need to make decisions. You therefore need to have characters that can occupy the same space while having opposing objectives, and it is the strategies that these characters employ in trying to achieve their objective that gives the piece its sense of forward momentum. If you create a piece that is not objective driven, it must rely on strength of character and humour to maintain its interest. It also helps if people can come and go, so groupings can vary but be kept to small numbers. Three or four are enough. As well as action between the characters, you are also looking for the potential for 'business' – that is, the small and seemingly inconsequential action that the characters indulge in, that is often a source of humour. The Commedia word lazzi is applicable here, routines of comic invention that go beyond the real, and yet remain rooted in a universal truth.

Imagine. Music exams are taking place behind a closed door. Chairs are grouped in the waiting area. There is much potential here. There are the examinees, singly or with parents. There is the examiner. There is the sound of the piano from behind the door. Props abound – music stands, lucky cuddly toys, an inappropriate snack etc. Music is dropped, forgotten. Somebody is trying to concentrate while another has their personal stereo up too loud. People go into the room in one emotional state and exit in another. How do people react to a perfect sound emanating from the room? Or to a disaster? There is much coming and going, and the examiner has a weak bladder. Hand injuries are always a possibility.

From these few simple ideas, it seems that there is scope for a short piece. The next stage is to make the masks. Several children, some parents, the examiner. You need to think about groupings, and design masks that create tension when put together. From wimps and bullies onward, you can often surprise yourself by what happens to people in unlikely groupings. Leaving even more open to serendipity, you could make a set of masks almost at random, and audition them for parts. The less that is written in stone, the more that happy accidents are likely to occur. It is important that all the masks appear to be from the same 'species' if they are inhabiting the same time and space. However, there could be many reasons for mixing mask styles, but these reasons need to be clear. For instance, Martians could land, ghosts appear, a dream or flashback could be seen.

With the masks made, the next step in the process is to explore their world, create the characters, using exercises laid out in Chapters 5 and 6. It is always useful to create the set for the piece early on, so that the characters are working and responding to a specific space. The masks need real things to play with, be it doors, tables, chairs, or a host of props appropriate to the situation. Here's an exercise exploring the potential of a prop.

EXERCISE: FOUND OBJECTS

Everybody has to bring in an object, without knowing what it is for. They then have to come up with three pieces of comic business with that prop, which can be done in or out of masks. While you are at it, see if you can get them to animate the object, find its centre of intelligence and its quality of movement. Every object will have its own unique way of moving, that is generic to that object. The speed with which it moves is related to its size and its tactile quality. Essentially you are looking for logical movement that lets you believe it has a centre of intelligence ie; a brain!

The process for creating an observation piece is very simple: lots of improvisations! Put characters together in different groups, give them objects to play with, give them clear objectives that they might want to achieve, and let them discover the strategies for doing so. Work in masks when creating the characters, but you can then work out of mask when working on the detail of the scene, the choreography, and even some of the impros. The best place to start the improvisations is with simple entrances, getting the characters to create drama and interest simply by the tension with which they walk on stage.

What you are looking for in the impros are the golden nuggets, the brilliant bits which make up, if you are lucky, only about 5–10 per cent of each impro. But by repeating the work, in and out of masks allows the actor to develop ideas, discard the chaff and concentrate on linking together the nuggets. The director's job is filtering the work, suggesting fruitful avenues of exploration, and facilitating a process that is ultimately led by the creativity of the actors.

Running gags and through lines of narrative are useful ways of pacing an observation piece, so for instance, if a character is trying to achieve something, rather than trying everything at once, break up the different strategies over the course of the piece, building in tension to some sort of resolution. Much of Trestle's early work, such as *Hanging Around*, *Plastered* and *Crèche*, was structured like this, lasting anything from 20 to 45 minutes. In *Plastered* (1984), the characters relocated after the first half to a different place, from a pub to a hospital, with the injection of new characters as the hospital staff. *A Slight Hitch* (1985) followed two families over the day of a wedding, though in truth it was made up of six scenes observing the characters in recognisable situations – outside the church, the brides house, the reception, the flight, the honeymoon hotel etc. We also found it useful to have the audience identify with one principal character, and for that character to undergo some change over the course of the action. So even if the piece isn't narrative driven, it still has the sense of an emotional and character arc about it.

Narrative structure

Devised work is usually guilty of bad structure. Trestle were very keen to dismiss this bad trait, and produce work that, though devised, had solid structures. Our inspiration came from television and film, from Dennis Potter or the story structure of Robert McKee. We took like magpies and applied theories and methods to our own stories.

Here is a simple way of structuring a devising process. It worked for us on shows such as *Top Storey*, *Island* and *Ties that Bind*. First, you need to create your story. Here are some starting points, with the shows we created from them in parentheses.

- Adapting books or films
- Starting from an intriguing news item (*Island*)
- Taking a historical incident or character (*Blood and Roses*)
- Build around a single or group of images (*Beyond the Blue Horizon*)
- Create a story from found objects
- Create stories from observed incidents or characters (*Passionfish*)
- Use myths or legend (*Adventures of the Stoneheads*)
- Take two-dimensional work, such as an artist's or cartoonist's work (*State of Bewilderment*)
- Biography (*Tonight We Fly*).

Break the story into the essential scenes that tell the story, and add some scenes that seem necessary without being essential. Make sure you have numbered them chronologically. Now stage these scenes as simple moving images – even still photographs. This is your visual narrative, allowing you to check that you can tell the story in mask and without text. It's a sort of storyboard. You may want to develop the scenes a bit, but don't do too much work.

Now comes the fun part. Do you have to start at the beginning? With your scenes numbered, play around with starting at different points and developing different structures. Use flashback and flashforward, see snippets of the same scene repeated etc. How can the story be best told to an audience, to stay on the right side of the line of obscurity and not cross over into infuriating obfuscation? Once you have one structure, find a different start point and come up with a different show!

With a structure in place, it is now time to go to the start and really work the material in each scene. Choreography plays a major part, in so far as people's actions need to be set at certain moments, to allow the other masks to function around them. Add scenery, props, music and costume. One needs to be clear about the conventions one is using, and how one jumps between both scenes and different conventions.

Staging narrative

Here is a breakdown of the process for the creation of a very successful Trestle Theatre Company show, *Island* (2000).

The piece started as a news item in the *Observer*, telling of the discovery of the remains of an old lady on a traffic island in West Bromwich. Nobody had reported her missing. She was well dressed. She had been dead for two months. I was intrigued to know how someone could live an entire life, and yet end it completely unknown, with no one to miss them if they disappeared. So we wrote a past life for this lady, whom we called Mildred. We used the idea that her life was full of people being parted from her, with Mildred finding herself alone for a variety of reasons.

Figure 7.5 Mildred and youth from *Island*, Trestle Theatre Company, masks by Mike Chase

The story of Island

First up, we see a happy family of parents and their children, playing at the seaside, in 1933. The young girl, about 7, finds a shell and her mother shows her how to hear the sea in it. This is the young Mildred. In 1938 she is evacuated, aged 12, but separated from her brother at the station and never knows where he went. Her parents then die in London in the Blitz. At the end of the war, aged 19, she is in the Women's Royal Naval Service, and meets and falls in love with a soldier, Owen. Owen's friend, Frank, tries to woo her first, but to no avail. She says farewell to Owen at a station, not realising her brother is in the same regiment, and passes him by on the platform. On the last day of the war Owen and Frank receive an order to secure a vantage point. They toss for it. Owen loses, tries to advance and is killed. As Mildred receives the news, she also discovers she is pregnant. After the war, Frank is already betrothed to another woman and says farewell to Mildred at his wedding.

Mildred brings the baby up on her own. She takes her to the seaside and shows the girl how to hear the sea in a shell. When the girl reaches 18 she goes off travelling around the world. It is 1964. She returns a year later with a husband in tow. They try to settle down with Mildred, but return to his country for good – Canada!

Many years pass. From out of the blue, an old man arrives in a wheel-chair. It is her brother. He has managed to trace Mildred after all these years. He is very ill, but they are reunited for a while. On a visit to the beach, as she searches for shells, he quietly passes away.

The daughter has her own life and doesn't keep in touch, but Mildred is happy enough. One morning she disturbs a gang of young tear-aways ransacking her house – they think she is out and have her radio on full blast. She stands up to them, and is bludgeoned to the floor. They flee. She lies unconscious on the ground. A man arrives, military in bearing, but leaning heavily on a stick. He searches for the right house and rings Mildred's front door bell. It is Frank, now a widower, come to seek out his best friend's widow. But nobody answers, in fact he can hear loud music inside the house. He thinks he has the wrong address. He leaves, and throws away the piece of paper with Mildred's details on it.

Mildred regains consciousness. She is scared now of her own house. She puts her coat and scarf on, and leaves, taking her trolley with her. She's not sure where she's going. Her scarf is whipped off in a breeze and crosses the road, landing on a bush on a large roundabout. She manages to retrieve it, but then finds she can't get off the traffic island. A hitchhiker arrives, they strike up some rapport, but the girl gets a lift before she can help Mildred off. Two workmen arrive, and think Mildred is a batty old bag lady. She befriends one of them, but he finds the rush hour traffic too heavy to get her off, and loses inter-est in her plight. Finally they leave, having forgotten about the mad woman who has clearly taken leave of her senses. It starts to get cold. Day turns to night. The same young hooligans storm across the island in a drunken frenzy, steal her trolley. The straggler in the group, a young girl, recognises Mildred. She feels guilty and sorry for her so tries to help her across the road. But her friends return and whisk her away from the old lady. On her own, all reason now gone, snow falling upon her frail shoulders, Mildred takes off her warm coat and dances with the memory of her lover Owen. She dies that night.

So the story we invented was about chance, decisions that are made that always left her on her own. We turned this story into a series of simple visual scenes, numbering about 20, with the last scene, the day on the roundabout being scene 20, containing within it many smaller scenes. This is how we broke it down.

Sc 1   Happy family on beach.
Sc 2   Evacuation at station. Brother and sister parted.
Sc 3   Blitz – death of parents.
Sc 4   Brother and sister reading letters about their parents' death.
Sc 5   Aged 19, Mildred at a ball. Meets Owen and Frank.
Sc 6   Relationship with Owen grows.
Sc 7   Says farewell to Owen at station. Misses her brother as he fills in a missing person's form for . . . his sister!
Sc 8   The death of Owen in Berlin.
Sc 9   Mildred receives the news. She is pregnant.
Sc 10   The marriage of Frank. We see the baby, and Frank's regret.
Sc 11   Mildred and her young daughter are on the beach.
Sc 12   The daughter, now 18, goes travelling.
Sc 13   The daughter returns – married.
Sc 14   The daughter emigrates.
Sc 15   Mildred is reunited with her brother.
Sc 16   On the beach, the brother passes away.
Sc 17   Mildred is attacked in her own home.
Sc 18   Frank arrives outside the house. He thinks it is the wrong house, and leaves.
Sc 19   Mildred comes round and leaves the house
Sc 20   Mildred finds herself on a traffic island. She spends the whole day there. People come and go. She never manages to leave. In the small hours of the morning, she dies.

We staged these scenes as simple visual images, discovering how we stage death, the Blitz etc. We added the ghosts of Owen and the parents into several scenes, e.g. Owen appears at Frank's wedding, because Mildred is thinking about him. Her parents appear beside her brother when he dies, and help him leave the stage. So the next task was to work out where to start. We decided to start with Mildred flat on the floor, loud music blaring from her radio, and Frank, an old man, standing outside her house, tossing a coin. So, scene 18 is our first scene. We play forward into scene 19, and then into scene 20, when she finds herself on the island. She meets a hitchhiker there. They are swapping photos when the girl gets a lift, leaving Mildred staring at an old photo of her daughter. We flash back to scene 12. Then on to scene 20 again and the arrival of the workmen. The work tent they erect reminds her of a beach hut – we see scene 1. Back to scene 20. The noise of a lorry's brakes sound like a steam train and we are in scene 2. Then back to scene 20. Then the sirens of a passing ambulance bleed into the sirens of the Blitz and we see a combined scene of scenes 3 and 4. And so it goes on, returning always to the present scene, with Mildred becoming more and more vague and disorientated, prompting more and more memories as she relives her whole life. When we reach scene 18, we repeat it, as we do scene 19, and then jump to the very dark night of scene 20. We then play out to the end.

Several things were very important in the staging of the story. Objects had a totemic significance, as they were passed along the generations, appearing and reappearing throughout the show. They help us locate who people are, where they are, etc. So the main seashell allowed us to age Mildred from a 7 year old to a 19 year old, simply by them both having the shell. The father's watch is passed to his son, who gives it to his sister Mildred to console her at the station. She returns it to him just before he dies. Letters, jewellery, photos, a scarf, all were important to us in signposting the complex structure. Second, music played a great part in locating time and place. Band music of the 1940s, or Mildred's radio playing hits from the 1960s, the 1990s, or the channel of heavy rap the hooligans tune it to. Music signified memory as well, when Mildred remembered back, the sound appeared first, like film, to lead us into and out from a scene.

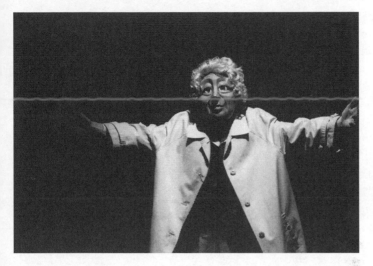

Figure 7.6
**Mildred in
her final
moment,
Island,
Trestle
Theatre
Company,
masks by
Mike Chase**

The entire show was in full masks, not a word spoken. The set was a simple round of green grass and two flats cut to look like the outline of a distant city, but covered in wallpaper. There was also a revolving arrow traffic sign that revealed a simple shelf in Mildred's front room, again to locate place. The workmen had a tent which they erected, which became a beach hut, a Punch and Judy booth on the beach, a ticket office at a cinema, a Missing Persons booth at a station, a bombed-out house in Berlin, and finally, when the workmen try to eject Mildred from it so they can go home, a metaphor for the way Mildred and thousands of other elderly people in Britain, struggle to stay on in their own homes as they get older.

The rehearsal process involved creating the coathanger of the visual scenes, coming up with an order, finding inventive and witty ways of going backwards and forwards in time, the segues between the scenes, and finding the humour in what was a pretty bleak story. We rehearsed in masks from day one, but did much of the choreography out of the mask. The idea of *jumping form* was always at the forefront of our minds. We saw visual 'chord' scenes, with several things happening at once, and repeated some scenes. We used slow motion, expanding significant moments. We brought characters back from the dead, and nicked an idea from the film *Gladiator* (2000) to portray death – the idea of the sound of a field, with buzzing bees and birds tweeting. There was less jumping form than in previous shows, as the story was a complex one and we didn't want to lose the audience. The show was originally produced in 2000, and was recast and toured extensively in 2002 and again in 2003. People saw it and loved it for being a 'traditional' Trestle show, being all masked, bittersweet in mood, and not afraid to pack some powerful emotional punches. For us, creating it, once we had settled on the story, it staged itself very easily and quickly, as we were using a method we knew would work, allowing us to think more creatively about the staging.

Here's a simple story that Trestle used to explore this process in 1986. Put the story through the above process

EXERCISE: THE KERRY BABY

A young Irish girl lives with her parents on the wild and desolate west coast of Ireland. She spends the day working the fields in all weathers, growing and harvesting potatoes. Strictly Catholic, she attends church regularly. She is aware that she is growing up, becoming attractive, but has no other life to explore.

One day in church she sees a stranger, a young man from over the hill. They meet after church. He is charming, debonair, and fills her life with excitement. But it goes too far, and she loses her precious virginity to him. Next week in church he doesn't appear. He is never seen again.

Her life returns to drudgery, pulling and scraping potatoes. But she discovers she is pregnant. She hides her condition from her elderly parents, until one stormy night the baby comes. She crosses the stormy heath and gives birth behind a rock. She suckles the child, and spends most of the night with it. As dawn approaches she wraps the child up in her shawl, and hurls the infant from the cliff into the sea. She returns home.

The next day, fishermen recover the shawl and find the grisly remains. The police are called, and the shawl is shown to people. Inevitably they end up at the girl's house. She is arrested and thrown into jail.

So, not a happy story, but rich in incident, character and atmosphere. It can be staged and broken up and told as you wish. Follow the staging guidelines above, and try to come up with different versions of the play – maybe assign the story to different groups and give them differing performance criteria, different forms with which to work, all the time encouraging people to break away from realism.

Robert McKee's story structure

Robert McKee is a Hollywood film writer who exposed to the world the way many films are created. His book *Story* (1997) explains the many ways stories come about or can be structured. It's a thick book, and can get rather confusing at times, but is interesting none the less. In relation to creating work for masks, we have used the basics of the structure, some of its inherent ideas, to create several of our shows. It is one more example of the curious link between cinema and masks, the oldest and the newest presentation art forms.

McKee calls the structure the 'classic film structure', a pure set of rules that produce a 'classic' film, such as *Jaws* (1975) or *Casablanca* (1942), classic in terms of their purity of structure and potential audience appeal. If one dilutes the structure in any way, the film edges towards either film noir or the avant garde. So *Thelma and Louise* (1991), while very popular, diverts from the classic structure by having *two* protagonists instead of one. In all other respects it follows the classic structure.

So here are the principles, and I believe they are there to acknowledge a way of making a story, but that diverting from the principles is not a bad thing, it just creates different work. I guess this might be slightly different from McKee's interpretation of things, but I have adapted it for theatre, and for mask.

The story is about one person, the protagonist, and the story follows them on an emotional journey, at the end of which they are changed in some way. This is the overall arc of the piece. The story is made of scenes that are in themselves little arcs, little emotional journeys – so the protaganist never ends a scene in the same emotional state as they started it.

Very early on in the story we have an *initiating incident*, an event that sparks the real journey of the story. From this event we set up a desire for catharsis that pulls us through the story. This is the way we can see the ending of the film hinted at in the beginning, and it is the journey towards the inevitable that is the pull for the audience. So when, in *Jaws*, the sheriff finds the half-eaten body on the beach, you know that at the end, he will have to meet that shark!

The protagonist has an expectation of life at the start of the film that may or may not be upset by the initiating incident. But soon there is a *crisis*. This crisis forces the protagonist to alter their expectation of their life and to make a major decision (remember, that's where the great acting is) and take on new information and new expectations. In *Jaws* the police captain decides to shut all the beaches at the beginning of the holiday season. Life then proceeds a bit until there is another *crisis*, and life again must alter – the mayor reopens the beaches. So we go from crisis to crisis – another person gets eaten, the fishermen go out after the shark in a chaotic fishing trip, we realise the shark can take out a boat etc. Finally we get to the *critical moment*, a crisis so big it cannot be negotiated, but must be faced. In *Jaws* this might be when the ship's captain is eaten, leaving just the sheriff on the sinking boat. This leads directly to the *obligatory scene*, the scene we've been waiting for from the beginning. The protagonist goes through this moment – the sheriff lying on the mast of the stricken vessel pointing his gun at the advancing shark, which has oxygen bottles in its mouth – and we find ourselves at the *resolution*, otherwise known as the ending. This can positive, negative or ironic

(McKee's terms) for the protagonist. So in *Thelma and Louise* it is an ironic ending, a mixture of positive and negative. They die but they are released in some way.

There exists in the story other elements, such as subplot and other characters. Of importance is the idea of *backstory*, an event in the protagonist's life that has a bearing on how they overcome a crisis, or the reason for the critical moment or the obligatory scene. A common theme would be a cop film, where at the critical moment the cop reveals the reason he's back on the beat is because he shot a kid once, by mistake. He then finds himself facing an identical situation.

We have created several shows using the classic structure as a starting point, and veering away from it whenever we want. We also apply the staging technique to the story, with heaps of backstory etc. Should you wish to explore creating work using this method, here is a brilliant exercise which I seem to remember was created by John Wright.

EXERCISE: THE CLASSIC FILM STRUCTURE

You need two groups, or if they are large, an even number of groups. Ask them to create the best ending to a story they can imagine – principally the *obligatory scene* and the *resolution*. They can use all the clichés they like, use any style, text etc. They need to stage it in very rough form. Then present the endings to the rest of the group, with each group taking responsibility of noting in detail one other group's ending. Then retire and create the *initiating incident*, the beginning to the partner group's ending. So they are taking someone else's end, and making the beginning. See how far removed from the end you can make it, and yet still see the end as a possibility. Once this is done and shown to the group, then start to create a number of crises that get you from opening to ending. Start off with three crises and a critical moment. When people get used to the idea, advance to more crises.

The trick with this exercise, or indeed writing using the structure, is not to be complacent, but to be as clever and witty as possible. Surprise people, upset their expectations, don't always go the easy route.

Text

When one is mixing forms, it will naturally occur that masks will be mixed with text. The pitfalls of this relationship are that, with their different reaction speeds, and the ability of text to explain quickly and easily, the mask can be seen as either very stupid or being like a recalcitrant child. If the narrative is too complex, the audience are working hard and sometimes crave the unmasked character to come on and tell them exactly what is going on. The relationship needs to be an equal one, with the text performers subsuming their ego at times to the needs of the mask and the audience, allowing the audience to watch the mask at their own speed, and not to jump in and continue the hum of text. As with screen acting, the text actor needs to get used to holding the stage, or playing minor to the mask's major, almost in a state of neutral. They can also maintain their tension level without speaking. In 2004 I commissioned and directed *Tonight We Fly* by Darren Tunstall, a play about the artist Marc Chagall. Chagall was the only speaking and unmasked character, with all other characters wearing masks based on Chagall's paintings. It was a very interesting process, working with a writer to create a script that in essence seemed like a monologue, but that contained within it the space for the masks to find their voice and their relationships with Chagall during rehearsal. Darren produced a 'production' script, an unfinished article that was developed during the rehearsal period, and continued to develop over the two tours undertaken by the company. We learnt much about how a masked actor and a text actor can communicate together. The actor playing Chagall commented that it felt very lonely onstage at times, not being able to look another actor in the eye. They were also aware of having to hold a mood without text while a mask played a scene or just a reaction, using mask-timing that felt very slow to the unmasked actor. What was clear was the generosity of spirit needed from all the cast to make the thing work. Although it was clearly a tour-de-force for one actor, it remained essentially an ensemble piece.

In terms of devising, there will always be a natural inclination to resort to the easiness of text, whereas there are moments that, if one

Figure 7.7 Tonight We Fly, Trestle Theatre Company, photo by Keith Pattinson

worked harder, would be richer without it. So here is an exercise, from Materic, that explores the idea of the *black box*, encouraging actors or students not to think that, if text is provided, then that is all one needs to think about. Remember the idea behind the black box – it is merely the voice recording of an event.

EXERCISE: THE BLACK BOX

Give a group of about five actors a simple set of five or six lines, non-sequitors that have no meaning if run together. Example:

'Hello'
'I don't think so.'
'Yes it is.'
'No it isn't'

'It's all right now.'
'Goodbye.'

The actors then have to create a scene of action and text, that contains these lines, in exactly this order – no changing the lines, no repetitions etc.

Encourage them to be as creative as possible, not going for the obvious, not running lines together or having a chunk of text and then action. Go for integration.

You can make up your own lines, and you can then be more bold, providing you have the time, to try to create a piece in several different forms, such as masks, text and action, or adding music to the mix. It is an exercise about the process, not intended as a way of creating work.

CHAPTER 8

Directing Masks

As stated earlier, rehearsing a mask to an empty room is a pointless task. It needs somebody sitting there to make it real. This could be another member of the cast, or somebody who carries the title 'director'. The chief role for this person is to witness the performance of the mask and offer positive criticism aimed at improving the performance. This might be a question of tweaking a gesture, timing, focus etc. The director must search for the 'but', as in 'That was very good, but . . .'. In mask work, it is often a question of provoking the actor to tell more and more of their inner monologue, and clarifying that the mask is saying what the performer intends.

I have been working with masks since 1981. Have I learnt anything? I usually find the best lessons are the simplest. When I am directing, I am looking for:

- clarity of thought and movement
- stillness, from which comes clear thought
- the moments of decisive or strong emotion
- the Truth, which is often in the detail
- the unexpected . . .

There are a handful of things the outside eye should be looking for, when watching rehearsals. It is very simple. The two questions you need to keep asking yourself are

- Is it any good?
- Do I believe it?

If the answer to these questions is 'Yes', then fine, things are going according to plan. But very often, in the smallest way, the answer is 'No'. How then to put things right?

Six reasons why the mask isn't working

The most difficult aspect is being constantly believable, in the moment, every single moment. Or at least giving the appearance of such a great intensity. There are several clear pointers that will show up any deficit in the believability stakes, and they are easily rectified. They will manifest themselves in several ways. The director's attention may wander. The mask may appear to stop communicating with us. We get lost. All this comes between the mask and a good experience for the audience. What usually happens, if the director is inexperienced, is that they will know something isn't quite right, but can't put their finger on what it is. So here is a useful checklist of what is usually wrong in an actor's performance:

- unnecessary repetition
- speaking without permission
- unsupported gestures/no inner monologue
- physical space
- mental space
- what!!??

Unnecessary repetition

This usually occurs when the verbal phrase and the physical phrase don't match. You need say something only once. When the audience have thought your thoughts, it is boring for them being made to think them again. Tell them everything, but just the once. Overcooking a gesture such as offering somebody a drink will sound, in the audience's head, like 'Would you like like a drink drink drink would you would you?' Turn that verbal phrase back into a physical one and you can see how annoying it is! Let the mask, and the audience, do the work. So long as you tell them everything, every little thought, but with great economy and clarity, they will stay with you.

Speaking without permission

When two masks converse, they hear each other by seeing each other, so that they can see the gestures and body language they are offering each other. If one character offers a gesture, and the other character doesn't see it, the audience will not see that character hearing it! Confused? Two characters, Dave and Jim, are standing centre stage looking at the audience. Jim offers Dave a cigarette, but without first getting his attention. Therefore Dave doesn't see the offer, and the audience do not see a completed conversation. The piece grinds to a halt. Simply, you need to clarify the focus, how to take it, with nudges etc., to guide the audience around a conversation.

Unsupported gestures/no inner monologue

These are gestures that the actor uses as compensation for not being able to talk. They come across as either irrelevant or meaningless, and are confusing and irritating for the audience. They are unsupported by a clear thought process, and have no clear text behind them. Clarify the thought process and simplify the gestures to correct the situation. Remove the mask and get the actor to talk the scene as if it was written as text. This will highlight the moments when they have nothing going on in their head! Gestures are not just something that happens when you move your arms. They are a major part of your vocabulary, so use them sparingly.

Physical space

Masks hate being crowded, and need a clear understanding of their personal space for them to work comfortably. Make sure the characters are in a good physical relationship with one another, with reference to the scene and the action. If masks stand too close together, the language they 'speak' becomes muffled. Again, we seek clarity, and part of that is having a clear space in which to communicate.

Mental space

If a mask is working well, it is constantly telling the audience things – everything it is thinking. But sometimes this can be a blur, and needs separating out, given more mental space. What we're looking for is more space around the thoughts. Some of the more important realisations and decisions need to be expanded moments, the speed and rhythm of the moment pulled apart as if it were happening at a slightly slower speed. This is to allow the audience to process the information, turn it into their own voice and hence to understanding. Don't be afraid to stop, slow down, expand moments and thoughts. It is as though, were the script to be written down, some of it would be underlined in red. Those are the moments that are expanded.

What!!??

Exactly! What on earth are you trying to tell us? I'm sorry, but I haven't a clue what you are on about. I have no understanding. This is a common fault. The actors think they are being very witty and succinct, whereas the audience are simply baffled. Take the mask off and tell us your thoughts, and then try to find a clearer or simpler way of saying it. Or are you trying to say something that cannot be said in masks – that does happen!

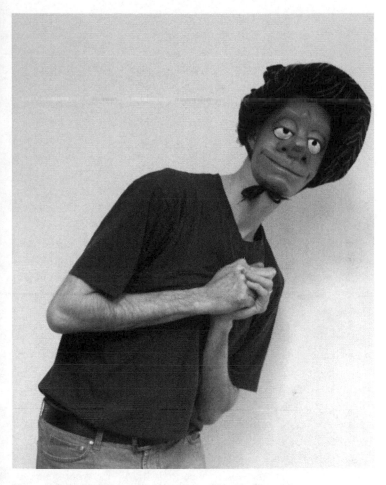

Figure 8.1 **Making an entrance, Simon Grover**

I'd agree with the adage that if you can direct, you can direct anything. For me, directing masks is about what Peter Brook calls his greatest ally – boredom! If the mask is working well, the viewer should be entranced, totally wrapped up in the character. As soon as the entrancement turns to boredom, something has gone wrong. Is it the energy of the mask? Is it the narrative or emotional logic? Whatever it is, it is vitally important to put it right before any audience see it, because they will feel the let-down by the mask losing its power even greater than you. There are many technicalities that a director must keep a tab on. Focus is vital. The audience must be guided around the stage, by whatever means, but they should always watch what you want them to watch. And to do that you must be clear about where the story is, where the game is going on. See it as though you are directing a camera – the audience – and you are making a great film. Identify the great moments, the dramatic points in the scene. Where is the build-up to that moment? How is it visually constructed? David Puttnam said that he had a response for every time someone came up to him and said they wanted to be a film director. 'OK then,' he would reply, 'a couple walk into a restaurant. Where do you put the camera?' This usually shut most people up, as they hadn't considered really what it is a film director does. And a film director works in much the same way as a mask director: you are creating stories, moments, atmospheres, through the manipulation of the audience's focus, and then by what it is you animate in that particular shot.

One mustn't forget *jumping form*. I tend to jump form when an opportunity arises to see something from a different angle or perspective, or to heighten an emotional or narrative point. Or if I get bored. So directing masks isn't that different really from directing text. One needs to create a working atmosphere that is conducive to creativity in the actor, where things can be tried out without ridicule, and where trust is clearly evident. This isn't a po-faced endeavour – rather the opposite. I think one should spend most of the rehearsal laughing and playing games, to encourage the actors, when masked, to follow impulses that seem to come from way off in their psyche, but that are rooted in the task at hand. Without those impulses the director will find it difficult not to jump up and say 'No, do it like this', which is always a crusher for an actor. I do find myself acting out specific choreography to illustrate a timing, but I do try never to show an actor how to play a character.

I'm often asked what it is I do when I direct a mask show. So here is a list of my principal jobs. I very rarely do blocking, as I prefer the masks to find their own paths, but I will tweak moves, and will also choreograph certain sections. If one removes the actual creation of the show from the equation – that's just devising, really – then here is an example of a director's job on a mask show:

- correcting focus
- clarifying dialogue
- cleaning up timing
- encouraging creativity
- expanding moments
- jumping form
- choreographing action
- providing music
- tidying up wayward gestures
- monitoring the boredom threshold.

Most of my mask directing has also been as sole or co-writer, so this will influence what I am trying to achieve in rehearsal, continuing the writing process. I have also commissioned scripts from writers, giving them either a carte blanche (*Tonight We Fly*) or giving them a structure to work on (*Blood and Roses*). Apart from the practicalities of getting the mask to work in the way you want it to, mask directing is just directing, a dark art that you can read about but never really learn about without doing it.

Process

The experience for most British theatre companies is of four to five weeks' rehearsal followed by tour. There may be the luxury of an initial period of exploratory work although this might be unpaid. It might also be devoid of funding to pay for the materials, designers and makers that might be used in anything other than a straight drama. So the rehearsal period can often be a fraught time of trying to travel the road as far as possible to discover as much as possible, while also being acutely aware that a paying audience will be sitting in front of it in five weeks' time.

With masks there is much to be done in rehearsal before the nailing down of the show can be undertaken. A homogenised style of playing the masks needs to be achieved – it is very easy for actors to play masks in vastly different ways – and decisions need to be made about the acting style. I would often have actors relatively new to masks working alongside veterans, so some time would be spent bringing people up to speed on their skills, creating a shared language of reference such as the tension states. We then have to make sure the masks are working properly. Sometimes, as with an observation piece, we have yet to 'cast' the piece, so we need to audition the masks for their parts. With a narrative in place, masks will usually have been made prior to rehearsal, so time will need to be spent bringing them alive, sometimes asking for remakes. Actor choice is also an issue. Occasionally a mask made for one actor doesn't work as well as it does on another actor, so casting issues need to be addressed.

Given the restrictions of vision, I have always endeavoured to rehearse using the scenery from day one. Masks need to be able to move confidently around their environment, without always looking where they are going, or stumbling about as if in the dark. Past productions of mine have seen the actors working on vast raked platforms, monumental piles of books and sets of rostra looking like rooftops. For the masks to work effectively they need to be comfortable in their space, so several days of 'set discovery' are carried out, with the actors working out distances, comfort levels, turning spaces etc. while in the masks. One foot wrong on stage could result in a nasty injury, and the effectiveness of the mask would be lessened if the actors are trying to find their footing all the time. On another level, if the actors have their environment from day one, their characters can respond to it in the way the piece develops. Too much theatre is rehearsed in halls with coloured tape on the floor and stand-in tables and chairs. The same is also true of costumes, although this is sometimes trickier. But a mask character is very much a visual and sensual animal, and will respond to how it looks and how it feels in the clothes it is wearing. I played the father in the original production of *Ties that Bind*, but struggled in rehearsal to get the character right. It was only when I inserted a very small cushion under my jumper and gave him a sense of weight up front that he started to gel.

The rehearsal process for masks is one of extremes, from free-form game-playing and experimentation to choreography and brain-numbing detail. If the first week is spent discovering technical aspects of the set and masks, and developing characters, the second and third week will be spent putting the show onto the floor in some way. A director should never attempt to block a piece onto the floor, but encourage the actors to play the scene organically, letting the characters find their paths, and then to tweak the action to suit the needs of the audience. A director's job in this period is also about provocation, encouraging the actors to create better and more material, to discover the 'live wire' in the production, to add music, and to suggest jumping form regularly. The director is also there as if they were the audience, to be a sounding board for the masks and to create something an audience might want to see.

The last week of rehearsal is usually spent adjusting focus, gaining familiarity with the new material and costumes. The technical rehearsal should be an easier affair if masks, costumes, props and scenery have all been present over the past four weeks. The actors now have to come to terms with working under stage light – being completely blinded – and most important of all, getting a sense of flow on the play. Pacing a mask show is a delicate skill: the masks want to indulge every moment they can but the needs of the audience might be that things move faster at times. What is important is that the actor has a clear sense of where the dramatic moments are in each scene, and that these are hit with the correct 'weight' to make the scene work dramatically.

In my experience most mask shows take several weeks to really play in, for the actors to become accustomed to the timings required by the audience and for familiarity to breed total confidence. A show will then have a golden period when it really storms, before curiously going off the boil.

It took me ages to work out why a show, once tight and effective, eventually became a shallower affair. The actors seemed to be doing everything required, still enjoying the show. But somehow, with the absence of text, the physical movement had become less vital. They seemed to tell the audience less, and with less conviction. But talking to them made me realise they *thought* they were doing everything, but in fact they had retreated into themselves, through the familiarity with the movement and had become less demonstrative. With text actors hear themselves all the time, can hear themselves hitting the right note vocally. But in a mask, the image that actors present is not known to them. I would endeavour to see a show, on a nine-month tour, every couple of weeks. Not always possible! But it was amazing how quickly the rot would set in, and all the actors needed to break out of it was to be reminded that they must actively be aware of telling the audience everything, and that it wasn't enough to think they were, but their bodies must register it as though the movement were text.

The fourth wall

How much should the full mask acknowledge the presence of the audience? I have already mentioned *clocking*, a very specific style where the mask plays off the audience for its timing, almost as if the audience were a camera. And there might be times when you don't want to acknowledge the audience at all. The problem arises when you are asking an actor to play an emotionally charged scene on their own. Unmasked, this would, for example, be a soliloquy. Masked, it can easily develop into a bad display of histrionics, looking like one of those melodramatic scenes from the early silent movies. To overcome this, I found a simple way of allowing the character to acknowledge the strength of the emotion it was feeling, without having to necessarily display it. To do this, we provide a chink in the fourth wall. As the character starts to feel the emotion welling up, they are suddenly checked by an awareness of the audience, of being watched. This immediately tempers the display of how they're feeling, echoing Peter

Hall's idea of trying *not* to show an emotion, despite the depth of the feeling. This might happen only once in a production, but the shock for the audience – of being acknowledged suddenly – only heightens the understanding of the character's turmoil.

CHAPTER 9

Developing
Time on Stage

Mask theatre was long considered to be only about short sketches, like classical mime and the world of Marcel Marceau. In developing mask skills, it is true that creating a short scenario is the best way of getting to grips with the niceties of the mask, learning about expanding into the restrictions and getting the best from the process. In creating new work for mask theatre, inevitably one has to consider a full-length piece – which Trestle did with *Plastered* (1984).

In reality, this first proper 85-minute mask play was two sketches in different locations with the same characters. Observed in the first half at the local pub, a disparate bunch of local gentry fell foul of the various evils of drink, and ended up at the nearest Accident and Emergency ward – from hostelry to hospital. New characters were encountered at the second location, but essentially it was two observation pieces back to back, the characters undergoing major turmoil along the way. It wasn't until *Top Storey* (1987), when we staged a drama, did we feel that we had created a proper 'play', made up of scenes developing a complex narrative and seeing characters undergoing transformation.

The main development in the work, which has informed all our theatre since, was the understanding about the depth and range of the emotional and psychological journey of the characters. The mask developed from being a vehicle for pithy sight gags, to a communicator of narrative, motives, objectives, subtext and conflicting emotions. The early work saw the masks interacting with each other in very simple ways – 'Hello's, do this, do that' etc. – and using objects very much as the source of business and the conduits for emotions. *Top Storey* saw the mask character, Stanley, an old man rummaging about in his loft and uncovering a nasty family secret in his memories, not only responding to the objects he found, which triggered memories, but also responding directly to those memories. He also underwent many changes in his various emotional responses to events in the loft, events out of sight downstairs, and to his own fears of being in the dark. Whereas the work previously was vignette in format, the new work saw the mask able to hold the stage for a good length of time, on its own, with very little outside stimuli.

Several things had to be made clear for this to work. First, the actor *has* to tell the audience everything that is in his head. This does not mean a constant brash declaration of emotion, but rather a steady stream of consciousness depicted by a thousand different changes of attitude, constant animations, changes in pace, rhythm and atmosphere. The actor has to have a very clear thought process – almost a complete text which, while it changes nightly, follows very much the same lines. The animation is constant, and the control of the breath is vital. Such subtle work requires the actor to communicate principally through the minute changes in the torso, which controls the breath, carries the head, and is the instigator of expressing true thought. Emotional truth, when expressed purely physically, starts at the sternum and works outwards. Imagine seeing someone you love walk into a room. The impulse for you to stand to greet this person will come from the chest, radiating outwards, finding final expression in the manipulation of fingers or objects in hand – clothes, hair etc. So the psychological journey a mask character goes on – and therefore that of the audience – is communicated by the continuous depiction of realisations, decisions and actions. If you were to listen to the actor's internal monologue, it would sound like verbal diarrhoea, but without it, the mask would not have the strength to hold the audience. And of

Figure 9.1 Top Storey, Trestle Theatre Company

course, if the actor does not tell the audience everything, then it will die very quickly.

I had an actor whose character kept on dying – going very still and not telling me anything. I got him to remove the mask and talk through his monologue – I suspected he didn't have one. But he did! It was full and detailed, exactly what was needed, but he wasn't finding the physical articulations, the little chuckles under the breath, the nods and shakes of the head, shrugs of the shoulders, that told the audience *constantly* what he was thinking. It was clearly rectifiable once identified, but it taught me a valuable lesson about how actors can think they are telling you everything when they are in fact communicating nothing.

Guideposts for developing the inner monologue

Michael Shurtleff, in his excellent book *Audition: Everything an Actor Needs to Know to Get the Part* (1978), proposes a series of guideposts to assist an actor in the process of creating truth and spontaneity in an audition. These pointers can actually be applied generally to the process of acting, and I have found them very useful in creating work for the stage, to add depth and substance to the mask's thought process. I started using them because I saw actors doing what their objective in a scene required of them, but little else. There were great swathes of action that, quite frankly, didn't seem interesting enough. Very little was being communicated to an audience because the character wasn't thinking much. We need to see them making decisions. They might not seem life-changing decisions, but the mask must consider every one, and demonstrate the process of deciding something and then acting upon that decision. So the guideposts are useful in encouraging the mask to give itself lots of decisions to make.

Of Shurtleff's twelve guideposts, only some are relevant to the mask, and they are my descriptions.

The moment before?

Let the masks be aware of what has happened before they came on stage. Where have they come from? What happened there? What do they think about the previous five minutes? Have they just left some other characters, offstage unseen, about whom they can now tell us their feelings?

Relationships

What is the mask's relationship to the other characters on stage? Mask theatre is nothing without relationships, so be sure to tell us what you think about somebody, or even an awareness of what the other person thinks about you. This may be communicated through your dealings with them, how you use objects while in their presence etc. It is never enough to just exist in the space. Fill it with thought and emotion.

Conflict

What is the essential conflict in the scene that is going to stop your character achieving its objectives? How can you make the audience aware of the conflict, what you think about it, and how you intend to overcome the conflict? Mask theatre without some degree of conflict and strategy will quickly become boring and shallow. If you think of the essential ingredients of the decision-making process, the *realisation*, *decision and reaction*, these things will obviously thrive upon conflict.

Opposites exist

Let conflict exist within the character itself. If it wants something, might it also not want it? A character enters to take someone out for a date. But it might also be nervous, terrified etc., that causes it to express a desire not to take the person out. The resolution to a scene should not exist until it appears at the right time, and the mask's thought process has to battle through opposition to reach a resolution. This is true for a text actor, but they have the words laid out for them. A mask must rediscover the battle every night both in action and inner text. Since all they have to work with is their physical tension, that tension has to be tuned exactly right, aware of the intricacies and juxtapositions evident within a scene to play that scene fresh every night.

Humour

This has nothing to do with the laughs, but the lightness of touch there in every character, the very human quality that makes us want to know them, no matter whether or not we like them. A sense of humour is critical if you are to play a mask scene that works with intense emotions. Seeing a character struggle with pain is all the more effective if we have seen at some point what it is that makes it laugh, or the light-hearted way it treats its own foibles.

Discoveries

Scenes are full of discoveries – discoveries about a character, about events, about the past. The important thing is to communicate the realisation of those discoveries. Expand these moments to give them their full weight. This is allied to the next guidepost.

Importance

Everything that happens on stage is important – otherwise why would people want to come and see it? The mask is well placed to communicate, through changes in speed and rhythm the importance of events. But it is not about working through the handful of big events in a piece, but about making the constant chain of small decisions, important decisions. Everything matters. Tell us everything.

Using the guideposts

In setting up and repeating improvisations, use the guideposts by asking questions of actors, reminding them of all that is available. It is worth repeating that mask theatre is theatre of the actor. It is the actor's responsibility to produce so much of the detail in the work, though at the time what the actor is trying mostly to do is not bump into the furniture. Repeating improvisations and concentrating on different aspects of the guideposts allows the actor time to flesh out the role and the action without being spoon fed by the director.

Here are some exercises that allow an actor to explore the fuller inner monologue, and whether or not he or she is successfully communicating it to an audience.

EXERCISE: THE GRAVESIDE

Set up a scene with a simple representation of a gravestone. The objective is for a character to come on and put flowers at the graveside. It's useful if it is an older character, the grumpier the better, but it can be done with anybody.

The scene could be very short, but the actor needs to find ways of expanding the character to fit the task. Who dropped them off at the cemetery? Do they want to be there? What did they think of the dead person? Is the opposite of that also true? What do they think of the flowers? How much can be conveyed just through speed, rhythm and tension? Can music help?

EXERCISE: THE GOOSEBERRY

A young couple are trying to get it on in the sitting room of their parents' house. Unfortunately a kid brother or sister is hanging around and won't go. The couple are keen for him/her to go, but he/she wants to maximise their pain and his/her possible gain. What are the strategies, how obtuse can they be pursued?

EXERCISE: THE LOVERS

Dance music is playing. A woman enters and sits down. A man enters and sits. They see each other, and know they are in love. At first it is just furtive looks, coy smiles etc. He plucks up the courage and asks her to dance. They meet on the dance floor and immediately the music stops. Embarrassed, they sit down together. Now what happens? How can they continue communicating? Does he have an object in his pocket, does she have a handbag? Does he ask her to step outside for a walk? Does she realise the time and she *must* go? Try the scene up to the music stop, and encourage the actors to devise different developments to the scene.

EXERCISE: DEVELOPING STILLNESS AND THE MASK'S CHARISMA

In pairs, choose a mask and take it in turns to hot-seat each other. Discuss the character, and construct a history and a life, a name etc. Write this all down. Then, in front of an audience, sit the mask onstage while the other person, sitting at the side of the stage, narrates everything they know about the mask. We observe the mask doing nothing, but hear all about him. The mask needs to be able to animate enough to keep us engaged, as though they are waiting for someone to arrive. When the text has finished, the mask can exit. You could sit the mask at a table, and place a simple object on the table. Repeat the exercise, with the mask being able to handle the object. It's not about trying to be wacky and invent loads of business, but about creating an inner life through stillness, and about pushing the actor to enthral us with virtually no material. The text acts as a foil for the visual image, sometimes throwing up surprising dichotomies.

Essentially, developing time on stage requires the skills of writing, devising and directing to discover what the strengths of working in a mask are and to work to those strengths. It is also about being open to developing your relationship with the audience, finding new ways of communicating with them, taking them on a journey that encompasses both mask character and their own imagination. Mask theatre can be about many things, but what it does best is people and relationships, so to make the mask work effectively over a longer period of time, the ensemble have to find things to say about these twin pillars of mask theatre that in some way are going to interest an audience.

CHAPTER 10

The Half Mask

The half mask is probably the most recognisable style of mask, particularly in its Commedia dell'arte format. The mask covers half the face, usually the top half, allowing the mouth free for verbal communication. They tend to be people's first thought when masks are mentioned, and they are a much misused form. Because speech is used, people think it is easy to knock up a half mask and slap it on the actor, let them run around a bit and 'hey presto' instant wacky otherness. But half masks, while a different discipline from the full mask, still require respect and skill and consideration of their application to be most effective.

Design

The principal feature of the half mask, the single factor that turns it from ordinary into brilliant, is the lip line. The lip line, when shaped correctly so as to give a strong hint of character and to work seamlessly with the performer's own mouth, can give a half mask an indefinable quality of 'otherness'. For this reason half masks are best made on moulds of the actor's face. While they can be grotesque, the eyes are generally in the right place, with the actor looking through them, therefore the lip to eye line is crucial for the mask to work properly. Noses can be as outlandish as required, and the eyebrow line is as important as on a full mask. You can also experiment with what I call 'three-quarter masks', which are a hybrid of full and half. They include the whole face and jowls, but the area from the mouth to below the chin is missing, just as wide as the mouth itself. The mouth line is fitted to the actor specifically. Thus the actor can speak, but on closing the mouth, the mask in effect becomes a full mask. A half mask does not have to follow a Commedia stock type; it also does not have to conform to the top and bottom design. There are masks that cover the bottom half, exposing the eyes and forehead. There are half masks that cover just the middle strip of the face, or sometimes just the nose. Whatever the design, the principle is the same. The transformation is incomplete, and is not lessened for that, but altered.

Half mask application

Whereas the full mask works best when it occupies a real world that is innately theatrical, creating this world for itself on stage at some remove from the audience, the half mask works best when it exploits its inherent contradiction. The audience are aware of both actor and character – the process of transformation is continually taking place in front of them, and it teeters on the edge of success and failure. This visual dichotomy lends the mask a sense of anarchy and chaos. We don't know who the actor is behind the mask, but we are aware of them. In fact, we are aware of two contrasting – and maybe warring – intelligences, the actor and the character. All this suggests to the audience a being that is somewhat out of control, on the verge of doing or saying something execrable. It is this sense of danger that is the half mask's principal feature, one that the actors of the Commedia understood and exploited very well. It is also this feature of potential abandon and freedom that has inspired so many artists since, such as Craig, Meyerhold, Giorgio Strehler, Keith Johnstone, Dario Fo and Brecht.

The half mask, straddling two worlds, also straddles two worlds in its staging capabilities. This mask is just at home romping among the audience, terrifying and appalling their victims, as it is onstage. The worst you can do to a half mask is to give it a fixed script to deliver. It needs to be able to explore other tangents, break out of structures before returning to the scene. Carlo Goldoni's scripting of classic Commedia scenario has always been seen as the death of Commedia, and a pale imitation of the art form at its best. But at least we have some idea of how Commedia worked thanks to Goldoni, particularly with *A Servant of Two Masters* (1745). And when this classic is performed by a top Italian Commedia troupe, you can really see Commedia working well. But ideally the half mask is about improvisation, whether you are just hot-seating characters in a workshop, letting them loose on an unsuspecting town in street theatre, or applying them to a loose structure and giving them enough rope to hang themselves! The definitive book on Commedia is John Rudlin's *Commedia dell'arte: An Actor's Handbook*, and much that he says about using commedia masks can be applied to the half mask in general.

If the half mask denotes something that partially covers the face, then one can also include in the general category the variety of noses available to the wearer. From the clown's red nose, to the Groucho Marx nose, moustache and glasses outfit, there are a myriad of possibilities. In *Running Dogs* (1994) Trestle portrayed a gang of dogs purely through the adoption of a black nose. In the Market Theatre's production of *Woza Albert* (1980), the white characters were played by black actors wearing white noses. Certain plays, such as Alfred Jarry's *Ubu Roi* (1896) or Goldoni's farces, lend themselves to half masks, as do some plays by playwrights such as Brecht or John Arden.

Using the half mask

The half mask is a simpler tool to use because the actors can hear what they are saying, so there is less confusion, making them easier to improvise in and more accessible to your average class of students or actors. So many of the usual improvisation games are applicable when starting to learn to use the half mask. A good starting point

Figure 10.1 Running Dogs, Trestle Theatre Company

would be the 'Yes, and . . .' game, or the 'Presents' exercise in Chapter 5. The same is true of the character work, such as the 'Centres of personality', exercise and the 'Pastiche' exercise. Here are some impro exercises designed to release the imaginations of the actors and to encourage spontaneity. Do these before you put masks on.

EXERCISE: THERE'S A FIRE?

Two actors meet onstage. The first actor starts with a pre-set line, said with full attitude and emotion, for instance, 'There's a fire!!' The second actor reacts by repeating this line as a question and adding his or her own. The first actor repeats this and then his or her own.

'There's a fire!!'
'There's a fire?!! We'd better run!'
'We'd better run? We can't do that!'
'We can't do that? We must save ourselves!'
'Save ourselves? We must get all the animals out!'
'Get the animals out? There are too many of them!'
'Too many of them? We'll have to ride some!'
'Ride some? What if we eat a few?'
'Eat a few? . . .'

The exercise continues as long as you want. The important point is that *there are no pauses!* Half masks are all about spontaneity and immediacy. Get actors used to thinking on their feet.

Having done similar preliminary work to the full mask, concentrating more on vocal exercises, the next step is straight to the hot-seat. Nothing useful can be gained from the half mask just by doing entrance exercises – they need the vocal release. After a brief period observing the mask in the hand and trying out different faces, the actor dons the mask and allows him or herself to look in the mirror. The next few moments are spent reacting to that image, adjusting posture and face to produce a sense of character, of its dynamic physicality. At the same time a voice is developed – just grunts or squeaks at first, as though the character is learning to speak for the first time. This will finally give way to speech, and the character can be hot-seated. As in the full mask hot-seat, never trust a thing they say, tell them they are lying, and find ways to provoke the extremes of the character, to ensure that the improvisation keeps its keen edge, and never just portrays an actor going through the motions with just a mask on. The half mask requires total commitment at all times. The actor should be sweating! The other thing to remember is that the half mask gives the actor a licence to say anything the character wants, and sometimes the results can be quite shocking.

Many vocal impro games are relevant to the half mask, so just play. But a particular skill to develop is the 'lazzi', where a simple comic idea is explored spontaneously onstage.

EXERCISE: DEVELOPING LAZZI

The first mask enters and establishes that it wants the other mask to join it, and in doing so they define the relationship between them. The first mask calls for the other mask. The calling turns into wheedling, fury, boredom, threats etc. – a calling lazzi – until finally the second mask enters. The first mask establishes that they want the other person to do a simple task for them – fetch some milk, make breakfast, rub their back etc. The second mask plays a simple 'Saying No' lazzi, forcing the first mask into an 'asking' lazzi. Eventually the first mask asks 'Why not?' This forces the second mask to come up with an excuse, which the first mask dismisses. An 'excuse' lazzi ensues. Finally, the second mask says they can't do the task because they are dying, and a dying lazzi ensues, followed by a grieving lazzi from the first mask. God knows how it all ends!

The temptation will always be to put masks on actors working on a straight script, in the desire to do something a bit different. Resist this temptation! It can work so long as you realise the script and structure are open to change and augmentation. Try not to stifle the half mask's exuberance by physical and verbal blocking, but provide structure for them to work around. Think of the anarchy of the Goon shows compared to the written script and you should get the idea.

Develop the half mask through improvised or structured scenario, using for instance the 'Seven states of tension' to provoke radical changes in direction, or to encourage game-playing. Here are a few suggested scenarios.

EXERCISE: THE FUNERAL

A number of characters are arriving for a funeral. Establish relationships, status, roles etc. As the priest commences the burial, people take it upon themselves to interject, through a series of lazzi. For instance there could be a 'revelation' lazzi where characters vie with each other to produce the most preposterous revelation about the deceased. 'I'm having his baby!' etc. Characters could also be envious of all the attention the deceased is receiving, and decide to try to upstage events with their own death. 'Death' lazzis are always a fruitful area. The same is true for a grief lazzi, trying to outdo the closest relative, all done in the worst possible taste.

EXERCISE: THE WEDDING

As above, establish characters, relationships, roles etc. The structure for a wedding is well known, so find ways of subverting or straying from the structure. Missing brides, drunk best man, lost rings etc. A good lazzi opportunity would be the moment when the priest asks 'Do you know of any cause or just impediment why these two people should not be married . . .' Characters could vie with each other for the most ridiculous reason. Half masks are the antithesis of politically correct, and the wedding is an opportunity for much ribald action.

Status

The half mask is an ideal vehicle for exploring the status of character, and theatre games exploring status exist in many textbooks. The improvisational skills of the half mask are well suited to the status games that explore a character's struggle against their status, their desire to rise up a level or maintain a level while losing status.

You can explore status through the numbering system, where 1 is low and 10 is high, or the playing card system, where ace is lowest and the king is high. Here's a start to understanding status, which is very much about how others perceive or treat you.

EXERCISE: MEET AND GREET

With about ten people, stick a piece of paper to each person's forehead with a number on it, covering 1 to 10. If you are using playing cards, fix one to each person's forehead. The important thing is *they mustn't know their own number or card*. Initially they can wander around greeting and talking to each other, responding to the number they see on the person's head. For instance, if they meet someone with a low number or card, they might be quite short with them, or rude, and a high number might elicit a bout of toadying. The middle numbers are interesting, because you have to have some idea of your own status, gathered from the way people treat you. This exercise can be set in a familiar situation – a drinks party, a family gathering, kids hanging around on a street corner etc. Finally, ask the group to line up in numerical order, putting themselves where they think their number is. Then remove the papers/cards and discuss how the exercise worked, how they made their decisions etc.

The masks can be used when a basic understanding of status games has been achieved. Put the masks into impro scenes where status is important, and where games can be played – characters pretending to be of higher status, or finding impulses that reduce people's status.

Again, an understanding of Commedia is an understanding of status, so many scenarios from Commedia are relevant, though you don't have to use Commedia masks.

Status archetypes

The status archetypes are useful for understanding the gradation of status in terms of character. Here's the ladder of status.

*   *The fool:* lowest of the low, uncomprehending, harmless, doesn't know they're the fool.
*   *The innocent:* wide-eyed and accepting, forgetful, sees the world as a baby does, with everything new and to be explored.
*   *The trickster:* conniving and deceitful, ruthless but not the brightest.
*   *The mother:* warm, generous, helpful and caring, sees the best in everybody.
*   *The hero:* brave, true, eager for martyrdom, accepting of their fate, a strong and noble demeanour.
*   *Royalty:* total status, complete authority, so doesn't have to show it, calm, assured, with total power. Imagine having a hundred people behind you to do your bidding.

You can use the archetypes to play status games and improvisations. Start by getting the whole group to find their fool, then their innocent and so on. Make sure they find both the vocal and physical quality of each level. Set up simple impros such as greetings in the street, people wanting something from the other etc. It is always interesting to put characters into situations that are higher or lower status than their own natural state – a high status patient with a low status doctor for example.

Individual actors can explore their own change in status. Here's an exercise I remember from college.

EXERCISE: THE PEACH

Take the highest status mask you have. If doing this unmasked, play the King. The character is then handed an imaginary peach – his status is evident in the way he doesn't look at the giver or the peach! He takes a bite from it, but it dribbles down his chin. His status drops as he tries to wipe it, aware that 100 courtiers are watching him. In trying to re-establish his high status, his status drops again, and this process repeats until he is a gibbering fool on the floor. Gradually he realises who he is, and slowly rebuilds his status until he is back at the top. Then he is given another peach . . .

Gibberish

A development for the half mask is to eschew natural language and work instead in a bogus form of speech. This tradition I believe goes back to Commedia and was called 'Grammalog' or 'Grammalot'. A modern psychologist worked out that only 7 per cent of the impact of communication was wrapped up in the meaning of the words. A whopping 36 per cent was in tone of voice and 57 per cent was in body language. Grammalog is all about that 36 per cent, which when allied to good communicative body language adds up to 93 per cent impact, proving its effectiveness. In 1999 I co-wrote and directed a production called *Beggars Belief* in collaboration with the Puppet Theatre of Kherson (Ukraine). We spoke no Russian and they spoke no English. We wrote – through interpreters – a complex folk story about a corrupt mayor and two fine clock-makers, blinded by the mayor so they wouldn't produce such a fine town clock for anybody else. The story followed their revenge, and was complex in its structure in that it constantly flashed back to tell the backstory. We performed in half masks, but how to communicate on stage? We created a language that seemed Slavic in origin but that contained only eight words which meant nothing in any language (*chourdah, booshoflee* . . .). The entire play was performed in this language, with much nightly improvisation.

The audience realised the game after about five minutes, though on several occasions people walked out after three minutes, complaining they weren't told it was in Ukrainian!

Grammalog can be used in situations when you don't necessarily want the text to be clear, or you want a definite 'foreign' feel. I staged a version of Guy de Maupassant's *Madame Tellier's Establishment* (1881) in half mask, using a French-sounding grammalog. The text is never set, but it is clear the characters are saying very specific things. For instance, in the first scene we establish the Bordello, as different men arrive. The women can say the most outrageous things without actually being filthy. It's all about suggestion, and much of the humour derives from the audience interpreting the nuances of the invented language through their own filthy minds!

With the following exercises, the first thing needed is to identify the style of language you are going to base the gibberish on – Spanish, French, German, Russian, Arabic etc. Start off by thinking of as many words as possible in the chosen language, including names of people, places etc. Then as a group – to avoid embarrassment – get the actors, unmasked, to answer group questions such as 'What time is it?', 'What did you have for lunch?' etc. Then work in pairs in front of an audience, in or out of mask.

EXERCISE: GRAMMALOG

- Two characters sit back to back and declare their love for each other. Unfortunately it sours and they end up having a terrible argument. They must never turn to face each other. Repeat the exercise with a different range of emotions.
- Two characters face the audience with microphone props (bottles?). They are sports commentators. Choose the sport and have one person commentating, then some banter, then the other.
- Two characters break into a house. They converse in whispers. One of them gets his hand stuck somewhere – the safe, the window etc, and then the alarm goes off.

Figure 10.2 Blood and Roses, Trestle Theatre Company, a three-quarter mask, James Greaves as Symonds and Paul Amos as Lambert Simnel, photo by Mark Dean

For a more thorough understanding of Commedia masks and the scenario, see John Rudlin's book *Commedia dell'arte: An Actor's Handbook* (1994).

CHAPTER 11

Other Mask Types

While this book is primarily concerned with the full mask, and the previous chapter goes into some detail on the half mask, other mask types exist that you might want to explore.

The neutral mask

The neutral mask has been much abused! In essence this mask portrays features that appear to express no emotion, character or opinion of any type. Skilled mask-makers such as Mike Chase have made neutral masks that can be said to portray a neutral character, rather than no character. At their worst, they are cod-robotic types with no dynamic stillness in them. A good neutral mask will portray a serenity, a stillness that can also suggest sudden or dynamic movement.

When you mention a mask to non-professionals, they will often think about the neutral mask and will be unimpressed. Many students want to use them in performance or experiment with them on stage. Oh dear. I have never witnessed a neutral mask working successfully on stage. They are usually imposed upon some dreadful scenario, used as a cipher for alien beings, or the id, or some other mystical claptrap.

But the truth is, the neutral mask is principally a tool in training, and not a performance tool at all. Theatre teachers and directors have been using the neutral mask in the workshop for many decades. It is used for a variety of reasons. It promotes stillness and neutrality, and highlights ticks and mannerisms. It encourages an inward focus for the actor, a pure sense of movement based on clear objectives, and both clarity and economy in thought and gesture.

Much of the benefits of the neutral mask are for the student observer, seeing how much the body expresses even when it is trying to say nothing. For the user, the mask offers the chance to explore the possibilities of speed and rhythm, finding dynamic qualities that can lead to clearer representation of character, thought and emotion.

Carnival masks

Trivia moment! The word carnival was used to describe the Italian festivals prior to Lent, and derives from the phrase 'Goodbye to meat', or *carne vale*. The most famous carnival masks are those seen at the Venice festival. The masks fulfilled the role of disguising the wearer, allowing for libidinous and licentious acts to take place, with no repercussions! Lower status people, such as servants, took to wearing them, giving them the chance to mingle with the nobs. Some of the masks allowed for speech, while others, with particularly long noses, allowed herbs to be carried in the mask to ward off evil smells and the threat of Plague.

Carnival masks are generally decorative, and do not hold the same power as a mask made for the stage. There are of course exceptions – the skull masks used in the Day of the Dead festivals in Mexico, or the animals and devils of Ecuador or Guatemala.

Utilitarian masks

If you define a mask as something that covers a face, then obviously there are many everyday items that exist to protect the face in some way. There is no reason why these cannot operate as expressive masks, and often have a haunting power inherent in their design. The fact that theatre is not their intended use does not diminish their power. For example, the blank face of the fencing mask, with its fine mesh surface, can have a brooding or threatening attitude. The gas mask can appear quite sinister, as can the welder's mask. They contain a sense of the alien, of something not quite human, that makes them compelling to watch when used properly. Since no overt character is evident, they work best with a neutral attitude, allowing for the mere act of masking to give them an authority and charisma. Conversely, they can work well with a strong sense of a character's attitude, exaggerated in movement. Naturalism is not their strong point.

There are masks that can distort the face, such as wrapping the face up in elastic bands or clear sticky tape. Blacked out sunglasses, wraparound shades or joke spy's glasses and moustache, all can be seen as an effective form of masking. The bank robber's stocking, the bandages of an Egyptian mummy . . . the more you think about it, the more examples come to mind. Finding a context for them is another matter, though using them on the street is a productive forum for the utilitarian mask, since the unsuspecting public are having to readjust to recognisable forms taking on a different life.

Fantastical masks

Masks in this category are easily obtainable in some form or another, usually around Hallowe'en. With the growth in books, film and television series based on both science fiction and fantasy – following *Lord of the Rings* (2001–3) – masks of alien creatures, ghosts, witches and wizards have proliferated in joke shops and confectioners. The designs of Jim Henson, the man behind *Sesame Street* and subsequent films such as *The Dark Crystal* (1982) and *Labyrinth* (1986), and a burgeoning market in computer games based on the original 'Dungeons and Dragons' have given children a plethora of creatures to exercise their imagination. No doubt their task is to shock, or in the case of 'Spiderman', to play a heroic character. Occasionally these masks can be used as character masks, but essentially they have something of the macabre about them, as do some of the carnival masks. But they are useful in interesting children in the idea of using a mask.

Object masks

Using everyday objects as masks has the creative tension of placing known objects in unlikely situations and giving them human characteristics. Occasionally one finds objects that exude a clear sense of character through a serendipic arrangement of features, but mostly they will give nothing, requiring the actor to create a clear physical attitude from their own sources. Of course one can manipulate the raw material. For instance, drawing basic faces onto buckets and wearing them, or doing the same on paper bags and cardboard boxes. The Swiss company Mummenschanz, from the mid 1970s, used boxes covered in fuzzy felt, with felt features they would take off and rearrange to change the expression.

As mentioned earlier, the colander makes a good mask, the base giving it a natural face. One can also turn everyday objects into masks by recreating them in other materials to make them wearable. Television sets, giant cameras, a vast chicken's egg – one is limited only by one's imagination.

Body masks

Sometimes it is possible to imbue a costume, or something that covers part or all of the body, with the same sense as a mask. The simple way to experiment with this is to place an actor in a sealed sleeping bag and on a clear stage see if they can project a sense of

Figure 11.1 State of Bewilderment, Trestle Theatre
Company, The Tower Blocks by Toby Wilsher and
Joff Chafer, after Michael Leunig cartoon

character. The European company Habbe and Mijk did something
wonderful by bringing a large duvet to life. I have even seen an
armchair animated. Body masks are usually seen on television,
especially in adverts, where cartoon characters are played by actors
in a costume. The Teletubbies are body masks, as is the Honey

Monster. Films such as *Star Wars* (1977) and *Lord of the Rings* (2001–3) are full of fantastical creatures that require a full body mask to operate. But one need not resort to a big budget number to create a body mask. Some street shows use actors inside wide flexible ducting, an idea taken from Mummenschanz, or inside rubbish bins. Try sticky taping newspaper all over the body, or plastic bags. Wrap an actor up in clothes. Using cardboard boxes you could make an entire box person. As with all these suggestions, the success of such endeavours is always in the application. A good idea needs to do more than walk on and off stage for it to work.

Other forms

Finally, the mask can take many other forms that still have a theatrical relevance. Here's a list of possibilities to provoke your imagination:

- masks worn on front and back of the head
- masks worn on top of the head
- masks used as puppets, disguising the body
- cardboard cutouts of photographed faces
- masks created to resemble objects, e.g. a car
- masks worn on the feet.

I hope that there is much in this book to enthuse and provoke you. I hope it arms you with exercises that will help you explore the creative world of both student and mask. The mask in theatre is a living, breathing form, limited only by the imagination of the user. Go create.

CHAPTER 12

Mask Design and Making

Design

The start of the process of mask-making has usually been taking a life-cast of the actor's face. This is a useful template on which to build the mask, to ensure that eyeholes are correctly placed, that the nose will fit inside etc. Under no circumstances should this cast be itself used as the template for a mask. The mask is required to be larger – or smaller as in Noh theatre – than the actor's face. An exact representation of the actor's own face would render the mask dead. There is no breathing space, no transforming space.

The inspiration for faces is all around us. People in the street, cartoons, paintings, photos, pictures in the papers etc. And then there is the unknown face. Starting with a blank half-balloon of clay and seeing what comes out from it is the most inspiring form of mask-making I can think of – probably because I'm not very good at repeating something I've seen or already designed!

What makes a good mask? Simply put, it must be expressive. It is as easy and as difficult as that. While it will show an emotion or attitude, it should also be able to suggest contrary emotions even at rest, and in movement it will be able to play full range of contrasting attitudes.

During the modelling stage, it is a good exercise to be able to pick the mask block up and animate it in the hand. What you are looking for are what I call the 'up' and 'down' faces. If it can be seen to communicate a positive and a negative thought, the chances are it will be able to show the ambiguities which lie between. A good mask will be brought to life differently by every wearer. A bad mask is one that appears not to change. This mask cannot inhabit the stage for more than a few moments. A good mask is not necessarily a beautiful one, with all the features present and correct, of the right number and in the right place. It can be a hit or miss affair, with no real ground rules other than 'it works' or 'it doesn't'.

Something to avoid is the sense that the mask is making a noise, usually depicted by an open mouth – a noise the audience never hear. Open mouths rarely work – though of course there are exceptions, so it helps if the lips are joined somewhere along their length. Another practical point is to constantly get down beside the mask and check its profile. Working the clay on a table, looking down from above, leads to a lot of very flat masks! Get down and view it from different angles. Pick it up (making sure it doesn't slip off its base board) and animate the nascent character, check its up and down faces, find a voice for it, talk to it. Mask-making is a good laugh, very sociable and full of surprises.

It can be difficult making a mask in a vacuum, without any sense of its immediate application. Early Trestle shows, which were full-length observation pieces and written through improvisation, started with a large group of masks which were then auditioned for parts, whittling the number from about 30 down to 18–20. We had a rough idea about character, or at least of an archetype, or a profession. For example, in *Plastered*, we needed a barman. Several were made, auditioned, and the most cantankerous got the job! Mask-maker Mike Chase often assigns titles to his masks, sometime in groups, making 'the elements', or 'the humours'. It was his idea to give a character a title containing a dichotomy. For our production of *The Edge* (1990) we all tried to make a mask called 'The murderous angel', to play the part of a beautiful but deadly witch. Several were made, but only one got the part. Other examples would be:

- the timid butcher
- the devious saint
- the sadistic doctor
- the defeated devil
- the saintly assassin.

Other design considerations include the size of the masks. The head needs to be able to turn on every plane with ease, so allowing the mask to look down, sinking its head into the chest, must be considered. Are you intending to look out through the mask's eyes, or maybe you want to disguise its eyeholes elsewhere? This can be done by cutting out the dark lines of the eyelids, the dark shading either side of the nose, or most simple, have the actor looking out from the mask's nose.

Homogeneity of style is important if working in a group. Unless this is considered, it is too easy for a mask to stand out as clearly being from a different planet compared to the others. Difficult if it is supposed to be part of the same family.

In designing a mask, there are few rules. But getting it right can be a confusing task. The most artless of people can stumble across the greatest of masks – Trestle's mask-making reputation was built on three Ordinary level and one Advanced level Art exams. Whichever way you go about it, there is no substitute for getting stuck into the clay and seeing what happens.

Other aspects of the process that need to be thought about before you start include the kind of abuse the masks are going to get. Papier mâché has a habit of absorbing moisture and falling apart if worn too often, and a plaster gesso can crack easily unless handled with some care. Using a vac form machine (which makes plastic copies from positive moulds) makes masks quickly and to a high standard of finish, but the machines themselves will set you back several thousand pounds! You can mix materials, making out of paper or modroc (plaster-impregnated fabric) and strengthening with fibreglass.

There are several easy ways of making the actual fabric of the mask, be it paper or cloth mâché, vac-form etc., but they all start with a clay

Figure 12.1 **Diagram of facial lines, by Toby Wilsher**

mould. So to start with, let us look at the process of designing and carving your clay.

The mould

The simplest form of mask to make initially in clay is the Basle mask. This mask is not a realistic representation, but offers up an idea of character, through the exaggerated features and unrealistic placement! Start off by making a half-balloon shape from the clay, several inches longer and wider than your own face. You can draw lightly on this with a knife the varying emotional types and play around with their placement on the face. As you can see, character and attitude quickly emerge with the simple arrangement of eyebrow and mouth line. These two lines, the magic lines, give us the essence of the character's attitude, its emotional state. But the simplest of masks can be just a nose. These masks have not, as Lecoq commented, 'quite resolved themselves into real human features'. The nascent character of the mask emerges from the shape of the face, the weight and placement of the nose . . . and that's it. It can appear lugubrious, alert, spoilt, devious, simply through the manipulation of these simple features.

We are naturally so adept at reading the human face that trying to recreate it naturally is fraught with problems – we expect to reproduce what we see. Unfortunately few of us have that artistic ability . . . and anyway, what is the point of making something that already exists! Far more fruitful is to make a mask that appears to be human but is also something 'other', which is a boon for those of us not very good at portraits.

Making the mask basically human means we need to have some simple understanding of the way the human face is made up. If you're really keen you'll get a book from the library on the musculature beneath the skin (e.g. Stone and Stone 2003). This is useful for understanding how features are supported, and give clues to the details that make a mask human rather than cartoon. It is safer to stick with the cartoon or caricature, but if you have the ability, then exploring a realistic portrayal of character can be very fruitful.

Here's a very simple process I learnt from Ninian Kinnear Wilson, a wonderful British mask-maker. From the half-balloon of clay, or a rough shape for the face you want, gouge out the eye sockets where you want the eyes to be made. The clay from this action is then put below the eyes as cheekbones. This simple act acknowledges a fact that most first-time mask-makers forget. The eyebrow line is not stuck on, but made by the bone structure of the face underneath – the orbis – so by making that first gouge, you place the eyes in their rightful place. You can then gouge out the cheek cavities, adding the clay onto the chin and the nose. This gives you a simple template on which to work.

There is no harm, unless you are observed, at staring at yourself in the mirror. Observe the distance between hairline and eyes, hairline to nose tip, from chin to nose, chin to mouth etc. Look at someone else's face and observe the profile of the face. Is the forehead further forward than the bridge of the nose, the top lip and the chin? Simple observation will help the first-timer avoid the pitfalls of mask-making. These include flat faces, bulging eyes, eyes that don't coincide with the actor underneath, and mouths that seem neither human nor cartoon. The human mouth is one of the hardest parts to successfully recreate, but it is easier to give a simple idea of mouth than to try and faithfully reproduce the lips.

Making the mask: paper or cloth mâché

This is the easiest way to make the mask solid and wearable. First check that the mask has no undercuts, such as a hooked nose or deeply sunk eyes, unless you are prepared to deal with a torn mask. Give the mould a good covering in petroleum jelly. Rip up lots of newspaper into strips – about 2 cm × 4 cm – and tear them, don't cut, as the edges blend in better. If you are clever, you can make two piles of paper, one of just ordinary newsprint, another in a colour, like the *Financial Times*, or a colour supplement. This allows you to know which layer you are on, using the two colours alternately, avoiding gaps in the process leading to ripping. A useful tip is to make the first layer entirely out of tissue paper, using just a small amount of water. This allows the mask to come off the mould easily.

Use PVA glue mixed in with a soupcon of water, and apply each layer with a brush, trying to get it as smooth as possible with no air bubbles. Don't use too much glue. Do two or three layers and let it dry, then add several more. With paper you need at least six layers for strength.

You could use cloth instead of paper. The benefits are fewer layers and a stronger finish but bed sheets or old linen can be hard to come by. Use alternate colours where possible. Three or four layers should suffice, done in one go. Dip the strip of cloth into the glue/water mix, remove the excess by running the strip through two fingers, and lay onto the mould.

Once the covering is well and truly dry, go around the edges with a flat unserrated knife and start to prise the mask from the mould. This can be tricky, and if it tears it can be easily repaired. Once off, leave the mask to dry out from the inside. When dry, cut around the edge to smarten it up. Clean the inside of the mask – baby wipes are good. Make the eye holes, preferably in the right place! Mark with a pen first to get the placing right. A top tip for getting the eye width right is to hold pen or pencil up to the face horizontally. Close one eye, and place the end of the pen right in front of the open eye. Open the other eye, shutting the first, and place the thumb on the pen directly in front of the new open eye. The end of the pencil and the thumb now mark the points of the two eyes, so put the pencil against the mask and mark off.

Depending on the quality of finish required, there are several ways of putting a surface onto the mask. It could be painted as it is, especially if you have been vigilant about getting each layer smooth. If you want a really professional finish you are going to need to put on a basic gesso, to smooth out the lumps and bumps. The quick and easy method is to buy from a do-it-yourself (DIY) store some Idendon, which is used in the plumbing trade. This thick white paste can be put on by hand and smoothed over with a slightly wet brush or sponge, or a damp finger. Otherwise, mix some PVA glue with some water and some plaster of Paris to make a thick paste, apply by hand and smooth out as above. Ensure that you work fast and that you keep the integrity of the features. It can get a bit messy, but that is half the fun. Paint the masks using your preferred paint, since anything will do, though I think acrylic gives the best finish.

The elastic can be attached with staples, or through a hole, though this might not last long when using papier mâché. The elastic should be attached about 2 cm in from the edge and level or just above the eye line. Attach wigs or hats as required. The thinnest available cable ties are brilliant for this – otherwise it needs a needle and thread.

Figures 12.2a–12.2J Moulds process by Russell Dean

(a)

(b)

(c)

(d)

(e)

(f)

(g)

(h)

(i)

(j)

(k)

(l)

Other materials

Modroc is a material used in hospital for making the casts for broken limbs. It's a plaster-impregnated mesh which goes soft when dipped in water, and then hardens as it dries. It is very quick and easy, though not as cheap as papier mâché. It is not so good at getting clear definition of line, unless you are very vigilant, and modroc can be a bit susceptible to cracking. But it doesn't require a gesso, as you just smooth the last layer out with the fingers or a wet sponge. Three layers will be light but fragile, and the more you use, the heavier and thicker the mask gets.

Drill holes for the eyes and elastic, but again, modroc has a habit of leaving trails of the fine cotton mesh hanging around so you will need to finish the mask off with a fine knife or some modroc as edging.

A very smelly and tricky substance, but quick and effective, is to apply a fibreglass paste to the mould, which has been coated with petroleum jelly. This requires rubber gloves, fume masks and a well-ventilated space. The material is a car body filler used in car repair, and Trestle's early masks were made exclusively from the stuff – the manufacturer even sponsored us! Mix the paste and hardener in golf-ball sized amounts and smooth onto the mask. It takes only a thin layer. Once dry, prise the mask off, clean the inside with hot water and detergent. It will need one of the suggested gessos, after you have removed extraneous strands with a sharp knife. Drill holes where necessary.

If you have a vac-former, place the mould into the machine (you shouldn't need to use petroleum jelly) and use as usual. Make sure you make air suction holes with a skewer or piano wire through to the base of the mask, to allow the air to be sucked out of all areas. Any little dips in the clay face, around the nose, eyes or mouth will need air holes put in place if you are to get a faithful reproduction. Cut round the edges, drill holes and you have a mask. To make lots of copies, you can now fill that mask with plaster of Paris and use the plaster mould for future pulls. Vac-forming masks requires that you avoid undercuts totally, and it is worth letting the clay mould dry slightly before you pull, lest you get some distortion of the original.

Mask-maker Russell Dean uses a strong vac-formed neutral face onto which to build the clay mask, ensuring the eyes are always in the correct place for the actor. It is also an easier task then to drill through to make the suction holes. If you want to do this, take a cast of one of your actors faces, make a positive mould from plaster of Paris, vac-form it in 3–4mm plastic as many times as you want, and use these moulds as your templates.

Negative moulds

Making a mask directly from the mould tends to destroy the mould. To give yourself a very smooth finish, and allow yourself to reproduce the mask, you can cast it with plaster of Paris, and work from the negative mould.

Line the mould with petroleum jelly. Build a clay wall 2 cm away from the edge of the mould, about 5 cm high. For tensile strength, cut up strips of hessian: the best stuff to use is called 'builder's scrim' and can be bought from DIY shops. Cut it into lengths of about 7–10 cm. Fill a bucket half full of warm water, and start adding the plaster – dental plaster is best, but not essential. Keep adding and mixing, up to your elbows in it, as it thickens and thickens. Knowing when to stop is down to experience, but the consistency should be like very thick yoghurt. You now must work *very quickly*. Place handfuls of the setting plaster on the mould, working into the crooks and crannies. Add the scrim all over as one would papier mâché for about one layer, as you slap on more plaster, then lots of scrim and lots of plaster. The mould gets hotter and hotter as the chemical reaction takes place that sets the plaster. Smooth the finished mould off and leave to dry fully. Clean yourself up. Let the remaining plaster set in the bucket, because it is easier to clear out when brittle. If you need more plaster immediately, for that or other moulds, then clean the bucket out under a running tap, preferably one with a trap in the sink to stop the plaster clogging up the drains!

When fully set after several hours, the clay will need to be removed carefully, so as not to damage the plaster mould. Should you have air pocket holes, fill them with some spare clay.

Selastic was a marvellous material, a chemical-impregnated felt that softened when dipped in acetone, and then hardened as the acetone evaporated. Unfortunately the carcinogenic properties of evaporating acetone were realised several years ago and the stuff was withdrawn from sale. So what to do with the negative mould? You could use cloth or papier mâché, forcing the material into the nooks and crannies. Fibreglass paste or actual fibreglass matting work well, though are not appropriate for a school setting. Liquid latex can also be used, if you have the inclination. If so, the finished mask will need to be supported inside with some foam.

There are cheap and cheerful methods of mask making: sticky brown tape, cut-out cardboard, decorated paper plates, painted cardboard boxes. There is a trade-off in standard of finish, but the younger the maker, the simpler the process should be kept. One can also cut out pictures from glossy magazines and mount them on card. Cut out eye holes and attach elastic, either with a stapler or through a hole cut in the side. The simplest and fastest mask would be to cut a simple template from stiff card, draw simple features on it – specifically the eye line and the mouth line. Cut out the eyes, and a section for the nose to protrude, attach elastic and away you go. For a more detailed approach to mask-making in schools, try Jennifer Foreman's *Maskwork* (1999).

Of course, all the above is for making specifically humanoid masks. But a mask could be made from any found object. I remember an actor at Middlesex University, Mark Bowden, who did a mask show entirely from such objects. They were highly effective and consisted of buckets, traffic cones and the central spiral cone from a top-loading washing machine.

No matter what style or make of mask you use, the basic principles for animating it successfully for an audience remain a constant. I hope you have found the ideas and exercises laid out in this book beneficial, and don't forget, the mask is nothing without the actor wearing it, who is in turn bereft without the audience. Mask theatre cannot exist in a vacuum, cannot be studied like a text. It is living, breathing theatre that truly finds its form only when all three elements are met: mask, actor, audience.

Figures 12.3a and 12.3b. Ristorante [12.3a] by Familie Flöz, and *The Chef* [12.3b], by Russell Dean

Contacts

Mask sets for sale

www.trestle.org.uk

Mask-makers

Russell Dean
www.strangeface.co.uk, www.thebluechicken.com
or
maskworks@btinternet.com (UK)

Mike Chase
Glasshouse Masks and Mask Academy
The Glasshouse
Wollaston Rd
Stourbridge
West Midlands DY8 4HF UK

Larry Wood
Fantasy Guilde Studios
PO Box 127
Crownsville
MD 21032 USA

www.fantasymasks.com

mummerdrummer@verizon.net

www.nohmask21.com (Japan)

www.arlymasks.com (USA)

Mask companies

www.strangeface.co.uk (UK)

www.floez.net (Germany)

www.horseandbamboo.org (UK)

www.boxtales.org (USA)

Business Unusual (Australia)
22 Sanders Street
Jingi
N.T. 0810
Australia
nickyfearn@hotmail.com

Training

www.lispa.co.uk (UK)

www.circomedia.com (UK)

www.desmondjones.com (UK)

www.ecole-jacqueslecoq.com (France)

www.dellarte.com (USA)

www.totaltheatre.com.au (Australia)

www.livingmovement.org (Austria)

Other resources

Try www.maskmakersweb.org for an exhaustive resource for everything to do with masks worldwide.

Total theatre network: www.totaltheatre.org.uk

Bibliography

Brook, Peter (1993) *There are No Secrets: Thoughts on Acting and Theatre*. London: Methuen.

Burgess, Anthony (1980) *Earthly Powers*. London: Hutchinson.

Craig, Gordon (*c.*1913) *The Mask* (a quarterly journal of the art of the theatre). Florence.

Foreman, Jennifer (1999) *Maskwork*. Cambridge: Lutterworth.

Hall, Peter (2000) *Exposed by the Mask: Form and Language in Drama*. London: Oberon.

Johnstone, Keith (1979) *Impro: Improvisation and the Theatre*. London: Faber & Faber.

Lamden, Gill (2000) *Devising: A Handbook for Drama and Theatre Students*. London: Hodder & Stoughton.

Lecoq, Jacques (2000) *The Moving Body: Teaching Creative Theatre*. Translated from *Le Corps poétique* by David Bradby. London: Methuen.

Mack, John (ed.) (1994) *Masks: The Art of Expression*. London: British Museum Press.

McKee, Robert (1979) *Story: Substance, Structure, Style*. New York: ReganBooks.

Oddey, Alison (1994) *Devising Theatre: A Practical and Theoretical Handbook*. London: Routledge.

Rudlin, John (1994) *Commedia dell'arte: An Actor's Handbook.* London: Routledge.

Shurtleff, Michael (1978) *Audition: Everything an Actor Needs to Know to Get the Part.* New York: Walker.

Smith, Susan Harris (1984) *Masks in Modern Drama.* Berkeley, CA: University of California Press.

Stone, Robert J. and Stone, Judith A. (2003) *Atlas of Skeletal Muscles*, 4th edn. London: McGraw-Hill.

Index

Exercises (Listed by sections as they appear in the book)